Kidmin
Leadership

Jim Wideman

Jenny Funderburke, Spencer Click, Jen Galley,
Sara Richards, Jon Warneke, Lisa Walker,
Larry Hillman, Kathy King, Sean Reece,
Derek Jones, Keith Warfield, & Beth DeLemos

infuse

An Infuse Publication

©2011 Jim Wideman Ministries, Inc

2441 Q Old Fort Parkway #354

Murfreesboro, TN 37128

www.jimwideman.com

* Reed, John W., *1100 Illustrations From the Writings of D.L. Moody* (Grand Rapids: Baker Books, 1996), 213.

Kidmin Leadership

Introduction:
Why Another Leadership Book?
Jim Wideman

Really? Another book on leadership? You've got to be kidding me. Aren't there enough out there already?

No, not really. Just like you can't get enough love stories and cookbooks, you can't get too much leadership help when you are involved in kidmin (*kidmin* is the Twitter™ hashtag used to denote children's ministry). You see, leadership principles are a dime a dozen these days, but help which specifically targets children's ministers and how they can manage the change in their ministries is priceless. That's what this book is all about.

I had no idea when God started dealing with me back in 1995 about teaching leadership to the children's ministry world all the wonderful doors and possibilities He would open for me. In September of that year, I was on vacation in Nashville when God first gave me the assignment to teach leadership to kidmin folks. I remember thinking, *If I'm going to teach leadership, I need to be the kind of leader others can look up to.*

My mom had always told me, "When you point your finger at others, never forget there are three more fingers looking back at you." So before I launched my monthly audio resource theClub, I knew I needed to be sure I was modeling all the principles I was going to teach. This called for immediate change.

I couldn't immediately change others or bring instant change to the organization I was leading. In fact, I still can't. But I can always change me! With every change I made, I saw fruit around me and in my own life. Each change in me bettered my ministry and my leadership abilities.

One thing led to another, and since I was already on the conference trail speaking at national events to thousands of leaders, I began to incorporate leadership principles into my teachings. I explained that children's ministers only work with one group of children, but their everyday duties involve three groups of adults: parents, adult workers, and other staff. A lot of the kidmin folks I ministered to didn't like the idea that how they related to adults had everything to do with their effectiveness with kids. Some told me they would rather learn about puppets and balloon sculptures, but every tool or teaching method has its place. Without leadership we are just educators, entertainers, or as I have heard it called "edutainers."

Whether you like it or not, your ability to communicate with parents and bring them on board to disciple their children takes leadership. It also takes scores of adult workers and volunteers to effectively minister to large numbers of kids. Leadership is required to be able to recruit, train, and lead effectively.

All of us who are working in a local church, work for at least one someone else, (many of you work for multiple bosses). We must realize it takes leadership to lead and to communicate the vision of the house effectively to many different ministries and volunteer teams.

Soon after God led me to teach leadership, in addition to conferences and seminars, I was teaching kidmin leadership on tapes that turned into CDs that have now turned into MP3 downloads. In addition to my leadership club (which, by the way, is still growing strong—check it out at http://www.jimwideman.com/the-club.html), I even give my teachings away free to kidmin folks thirty years old and under. Once the teachings began, I started writing books, and then I even added a blog (www.jimwidemanblog.com). Along the way also came consulting and doing some one-on-one individualized coaching.

In late 2006, God told me another piece of the plan for my life that has been the most fruitful and also the most rewarding to me personally. During the Thanksgiving holidays, as I was taking a little time reflecting over my life and ministry, I heard within my spirit these words: "There are things that you know you have learned from me that you will spend the rest of your life teaching to the next generation of ministry leaders." These words began to burn within my heart, and they began the largest shift in my ministry to date. This shift eventually led to a change of location and my role in the body of Christ. The more I prayed it out, as wonderful as conferences are, I began to realize they could not bring the life change that walking together with a group of leaders over several months or years would bring.

This quest for how to take the things God has taught me in the past thirty-five years and impart them into those who are willing to learn in much less than thirty-five years, led to creating and now evolving my Infuse Coaching (http://www.jimwideman.com/infuse.html).

The *New Oxford American Dictionary* defines *infuse* as: "to instill a quality or skill in someone or something; to soak or pour into." This is what I wanted to do. I had been asking the Lord to show me a way to pour into others what has taken me years to learn, so those leaders can be better leaders and accomplish more in less time.

As this ministry evolved, I realized I would have to limit it to twenty select candidates. So I put it out there, and much to my surprise, twenty people signed up to be a part of the first group. I saw from the beginning that every one of those original twenty had different reasons and expectations for being a part of Infuse. When I told my family that I was going to select twenty kidmin folks from all over the country and teach them by conference calls and a special website, they thought that was great. But when I told them they were going to come to our house two different times for a retreat here in Murfreesboro, Tennessee, they thought I had lost my ever-loving mind.

"How are you going to make sure they are not weird?" I remember one of my daughters asking. After I explained the application and video interview process, they all relaxed; but I could tell before, and even during that first retreat, my family trusted me and trusted God, but it was a real step of faith for them to see how all this was going to work out.

Sure enough, the first retreat came and went, and I was surprised at my family's responses. We were all sitting around processing the events and happenings of the last few days, and to my surprise, the same daughter who asked me how was I going to be able to tell if they were weird said, "Dad, by far this is the best thing you have ever done to help people!" It was just amazing. At the time of this writing, I am just completing my twelfth retreat.

After I did that first retreat, I was so pumped I decided to start a new Infuse group every six months. This is how I roll. If one group is good, having two or three or four groups is better. I am such a relational guy I just didn't want to say no to the relationships I had formed. So one year turned into two, and it was so hard for me to not add on a third year. But the cool thing is four of the original twenty are helping me coach the new groups.

Fast forward to today. I have now come up with a balance of coaching and offering Infuse only from September to February each year. This allows me time to concentrate on the other aspects of Jim Wideman Ministries like writing books, speaking, etc.

As I do life with these amazing kidmin leaders God brought together, I'm beginning to realize they have taught me as much as I have taught them. This iron-sharpening-iron stuff really works. So I started discussing with my second-year Infuse 1 participants what our next step would be—writing a book.

You should have heard all the excuses I got. "Who's going to buy a book written by everyday kidmin folks like us?" I said, "Everyday kidmin leaders who want to learn practical steps just like you do!"

Once they calmed down, they started answering the main question I posed to them: what are the two greatest things you have learned while walking with me these past two years that you wish you had known before Infuse? As the answers started to flow, I asked them to break them down into three categories:

1. Why is this important?
2. What do you do to practice this truth?
3. How do you lead or manage change to bring this to pass in your ministry?

When they began outlining their answers, they began to see what you will soon read—this book can be very helpful to a lot of people. The contributors of this book are some of the finest kidmin leaders I have ever known. During the writing process, it was so good to watch these leaders grow to a brand-new leadership level.

Each author in this book is on my leaders-to-watch list. Every lesson is a must for those who want to become better kidmin leaders. This will be the first of many Infuse books because kidmin folks like you need to hear from learners and doers, not writers and people telling you what they used to do in kids ministry.

At the end of this book is a bio about each one of these leaders. I hope you'll continue to learn from them because the truth for all of us is there are things we don't yet know. If you will be open and honest and hunger to be a better leader, that will force you to be a better learner as well. My wish is that you become a student of leadership and join me in a lifestyle of learning.

After years of watching children's ministry leaders fail to see their dreams come true, I noticed a common denominator. Most workers and leaders in the local church don't see the need to continually learn. To me, learning is not something I have an option of doing. It is a must. Being a learner must be a part of your everyday life if you are serious about growing.

When I was in college, I learned the smartest and most intelligent response to any question or situation is "I don't know." There's nothing wrong with not knowing it all, and I don't understand why people think it's wrong to say, "I don't know." The key is to let "I don't know" move you to "I'll find out."

In 1990, when I moved to my new church in Tulsa, it was basically the same size as my three previous churches. But as the church grew in the seventeen years I was there, every Sunday I went to church, that was the largest church I had ever been a part of. I didn't know how to do what I was being asked to do every weekend, but that forced me to explore and learn.

The intensity of how you pursue exploring and learning is the true sign that sets you apart as a leader. Study makes work approved. One of my favorite Scriptures is 2 Timothy 2:15 KJV, "Study to shew thyself approved unto God, a workman that needeth not to be ashamed, rightly dividing the word of truth."

Approved work is a direct result of study, and it causes the workman to have no reason to be ashamed. We all know hard work pays off, but smart work is also important. Smart work comes from studying and learning. When smart work and hard work are combined, great things happen. Smart work plus hard work always equals success.

If you are reading this book, I know you want to bear fruit and be successful for the Lord, but your actions measure the intensity and passion of that quest. In evaluating my own journey, I'd like to give you **ten learning habits** I believe you should develop to stay fresh and current as a leader.

1. Develop a love for reading. I'm always on the lookout for a good book. I look for recommendations from people I look up to. I visit local book-stores and peruse the business and leadership sections. I like to discuss what I'm reading with people who are also reading that same book. I'm also a believer in re-reading a book and making sure I've put to use what I've already learned before I move on to a new book. It helps me to set a goal for a set time to complete a book. To meet that timeline, I try to keep a book with me at all times. I also buy one or two books ahead of time so I'll have something to look forward to reading. It also helps me finish the book I'm currently reading as I anticipate reading the new one.

I've also enjoyed blogging. There are some great blogs out there. I like to see who has linked to my blog; I follow the link and see who else they read, and I check them out as well. I have discovered some great learners to learn with.

2. Listen to teaching. We live in a wonderful time. There are so many teachings available to us from MP3s, podcasts, and CDs. A great habit to cause you to learn is to regularly feed on information. I love my iPhone™ and iPad™ because I can keep teachings with me at all times. (You can also download my free app for the iPhone™ and iPad™ at www.jimwideman.com. These apps now have a player so you can keep all of my theClub teachings with you at all times.) Another plus to listening to teachings is that you can re-listen to them easier than you can re-read a book. Re-listening helps me process and learn the information faster.

3. Ask questions. This is my favorite way to learn. Jesus was the master of teaching and encouraging learning by questions. A growing faith is a questioning faith. I think fear of asking something dumb keeps us from taking advantage of this priceless method of learning. I believe with all my heart there is no such thing as a dumb question (there are dumb answers but no dumb questions if the questions are from a sincere desire to learn).

Any time you are with another leader that you value, you should take advantage of the opportunity to learn from him/her. Prepare questions ahead of time and put them in order of importance. That way if you only have time for one or two, you will get what you need. I get excited when someone pulls out a list of questions they want to ask me, but I have to admit this is not the norm. Most people don't view question-and-answer times as seriously as I do. It disappoints me when I conduct a Q&A session and no one prepares a list of questions.

Make a phone appointment with people you want to learn from, and pick their brain on a subject you need to learn about. Tell what the subject or purpose of the call is when you set it up, and always email or fax your questions ahead of time. When you email a question, only email one question at a time. Never email more than one question per week.

4. Develop a relationship with people you esteem. Years ago when I started in ministry, finding other children's pastors was not an easy task. There weren't many of us out there, so when I heard of another, I'd give him a call. Also, if I read an article that intrigues me, I contact the author. I still email and call children's pastors and introduce myself, and I try to develop relationships with those I want to know. When I see a hunger in other children's pastors, it gets my attention and causes me to draw close to them.

Watch out for relationships that don't sharpen you. I am so thankful for the friendships I have both new and old that God uses to cause me to keep thinking and growing.

5. Use your lunches and dinners wisely. A lunch meeting is a great time to put into others. I love to brainstorm over a meal with people I enjoy. I use the drive to the restaurant to set the tone or agenda, and I use the drive back to recap and make sure people understand the assignment or plan of action. A dinner meeting is my favorite way to connect with new people I want to know and learn from. Remember, the worst they can say is no. Also it's not about the food, it's about learning and brain-picking. There have been times when I have eaten before I met someone for a meal so I could take full advantage of my time to learn or teach.

6. Visit other churches. I love to tour churches wherever I go; and when I do, I take lots of pictures. There are several churches I've visited more than once, and every time I've gone, I've picked up different ideas. I love to visit churches with multiple locations and see what changes they made when they had a chance to redo their children's space. It's very eye-opening to see first-hand what others do. Get outside your church, and take a road trip to visit churches with creative and unique children's ministries. See what you can learn.

7. Go to conferences. I love to attend conferences for many more reasons than the sessions. I love to hear and see what has worked for others. I like to take others along with me to expose them to bigger thinking. A picture is worth a thousand words. When others go to conferences that I did not attend, I try to identify what they saw and learned so I can learn through them.

8. Network. Surround yourself with peers you respect. Identify the ministry models available, and find out what they are presently thinking. Just because you heard them once, doesn't mean you know what they are thinking and saying today. I want to know what and why any other person who has my position is doing. Sometimes knowing what not to do is just as important as knowing what to do. Always be on the lookout to find others who will discuss what they are learning. Seek to understand thinking different than your own.

Be a fly on the wall, and listen to others as they discuss and network. A few years ago I had the opportunity to have dinner with renowned children's ministers Sue Miller and Craig Jutila. It was a wonderful time of learning and growing for me. As we were discussing our ministries, I was so proud of all the other children's pastors who were attending that event and had pulled up chairs so they could listen and learn as well.

9. Study successful people. I'm a huge fan of the TV series *The Apprentice*. I love to learn from watching others lead. I also enjoy reading the life stories of successful business people. Those kinds of books are my favorite. I also love to brainstorm or chat with others who also are fans.

10. Get a leadership coach, or hire a consultant to hold you accountable and make you learn. A view from another perspective can give you a huge advantage. If you are interested in coaching, be sure to check out Infuse at www.jimwideman.com/infuse.

How can you make all of these things a part of your lifestyle? The best way I know is to get out your calendar and plan. Set appointments and then do them. We all keep our appointments once we make them. Develop good learning habits, and repeat the same actions until they become reflexive or second nature. Here are some of the places and situations where I like to keep books and MP3s available: the treadmill and other exercise equipment; on my nightstand so I can read right before bedtime; in the restroom at home and at work; on a planes; in the car; and I even take a book with me for while I wait to get my hair cut or to see the doctor. I make appointments with myself to study and grow on a regular basis.

Remember, studying and learning doesn't have to be all at once. Do it a little at a time, and expect those around you to learn. I ask all my staff to include on their weekly report what they have done for leadership development in the past week. You can't expect what you don't model, so why not make an intentional decision to set the pace and become an example of one who is always learning? It's up to you to stay fresh and current in your leadership skills and thinking. A growing leader is a learner!

Enjoy these chapters and leadership lessons. I hope you'll find ways to apply all of them to your kidmin leadership.

Chapter 1:
Right Leader, Right Place, Right Time
Jon Warneke

When I felt God was leading me to work with children, I jumped at the chance. I was all of twenty years old, in a small church, and taking a year off from college. There were three ministry opportunities open at different times of the week: Sunday school, kids' church, and Wednesday-night ministry. Which one did I want? Not knowing any different or better, I took all three. I loved them all, and I found out I was good at working with children. I was given gifts and abilities to speak into these children's lives and connect with them. I had never felt more fulfilled in my life.

However, God had bigger plans. Although I enjoyed and thrived working with and teaching children, I was really uncertain when God began to lead me to become a children's pastor.

Minister to kids?

YES!

Lead CHILDREN'S MINISTRY?

Why me?

I asked God, "Are you sure you have the right guy?"

I was uncertain and inexperienced with leading peers, much less *real* adults. I felt like I was living the line from the Queen song, "Bohemian Rhapsody," "He's just a poor boy from a poor family, spare him his life from this monstrosity."

Rest assured, if you have ever felt like me, you are in good company. We share a similar résumé with ordinary people like Gideon and Isaiah—God not only used them, but they also were great leaders. We read in Judges 6:15 that when God asked Gideon to save Israel from the Midianite's hands, Gideon was very insecure and, in his mind, ill-prepared. Gideon prayed, "But how can I save Israel? My clan is the weakest in Manasseh, and I am the least in my family."

His uncertainty and feelings of inadequacy were based on fact. After all, who could possibly fulfill the extraordinary destiny that God asked Gideon to pursue? The responsibility was enormous, the task was ominous, and the future was unknown. Wait a second. That's exactly how I (and many others) feel in regards to ministry: I can help God, but I can't lead.

Gideon was the right leader in the right place at the right time. If you are a ministry leader in a ministry position, you have to understand it is God who put you there. It is not an accident. It is divine purpose. Your experience being placed in your current position was probably not nearly as dramatic as these biblical examples, but God's plan for you is no less purposeful. Knowing you are right where God wants you to be is the key.

If you are struggling with being the leader God has already called you to be, take heart. There are **four leadership roadblocks** that threaten to hold every leader back, but there are ways to effectively deal with them.

Fear & Doubt: When an angel of the Lord appeared to Gideon, Gideon was hiding in a winepress. Similarly, many kinds of fear have held me back from being the leader God called me to be—fear of failure, people, letting others down, and rejection (for me the greatest of these is the fear of failure). But living in fear causes us to be inactive. The fear of the Midianites froze the leaders of Israel and caused inactivity. That inactivity caused the slavery and oppression of the Israeli people. Many times in my life, fear froze me, and I allowed my fear to overpower my calling to lead. My inactivity resulted in the same outcome as the leaders of Israel—people perishing where there is no vision and leadership.

Doubt works hand in hand with fear. Gideon doubted God's presence with Israel. We know this because Gideon clearly had doubt-filled questions in response to God's instructions. (Judg. 6:13.) Doubt is based in fear and experience. I, too, have many doubts. I doubt my own abilities and ideas, but God's declaration over Gideon rings true for each of us, "The Lord is with you, mighty warrior" (v. 12).

The Lord is with you—that is a promise we hear so frequently that oftentimes we fail to apply it to our lives, our fears, and our doubts. Simply, God promises to be with you. I hold on to this promise every day. I know God has placed me here to lead; therefore, I know He is with me. What more do I need? You, too, should operate daily in that promise.

For some it may be hard to identify with being called a "mighty warrior." You might not think of yourself as a mighty warrior, Gideon didn't. God was really prophesying over Gideon, declaring what God saw Gideon to be in the future. God prophesies the same over you and me. When I face fear and doubt, I recall the fact that God has called me to be a children's pastor and a leader of people. You and I can rest in His promise that He is with us, and we can boldly step out as mighty warriors, fulfilling the words God has already spoken over our lives and ministries.

Inadequacy & Insecurity: I totally identify with Gideon's response to the angel of the Lord: "How can I save Israel? My clan is the weakest …and I am the least" (Judg. 6:15). I grew up on a ranch where there were lots of animals and few people (only my family). The problems I was trained to deal with as a child don't translate well to the church world. For example, "Get right back on after you get bucked off" is definitely a life lesson, but it is a lot easier getting back on a mean horse than it is confronting mean people in love.

Growing up, if I had a conversation, it was with myself. I now live in a world where I interact with people on a daily basis, and every decision I make affects those people. I often feel like Gideon, "God, I am not the right person for this job."

God's response to Gideon's insecurity was twofold. He said, "I will be with you," and "You will strike down all the Midianites" (v. 16). We need to be reminded as well—God is with us.

Not only did God promise to be with Gideon, but He also specifically told Gideon that he would strike down the Midianites. God didn't say, "Tomorrow I will annihilate the Midianites with My huge hand." No, God said, "You will strike down all the Midianites." That was a huge and dangerous job that Gideon had to initiate, lead, and follow through on.

It is the same for us as leaders in ministry. God has called us to a huge and dangerous job. He asks us to initiate, lead, and follow through. If you are looking for someone else to do it; stop looking and start leading. There is no one else that has been called to do your job—you are the leader of the children's ministry.

I'm sure you have hit other roadblocks that have kept you from being the leader God intends for you to be. Whatever personal shortcomings or external circumstances are holding you back, it is imperative to remember that faith is key. Personal faith is a tricky thing. It is not static, and it has a habit of escaping us when we need it the most. But God is aware of our human limitations. When Gideon asked for a sign, God gave it to him. In the course of Judges 6, Gideon asks God three times for confirmation. Gideon did this because he was not in the habit of exercising his faith.

Children's ministry leaders have plenty of opportunities to exercise their faith. If you are stuck in a rut, frozen in fear, or feel totally inadequate and insecure; exercise your faith and step out and lead. It won't feel natural, but the results won't be either. Where faith is exercised, we must expect the supernatural.

Stepping out and leading begins internally. For a person to move past the leadership roadblocks, he or she must embrace what God sees them as—a leader. I had been a children's pastor at my current position for about two years when I really began to deal with doubts, fears, and insecurities concerning my ability to lead. At that time I met with one of my key leaders. After we wrapped up the meeting, he looked at me and said, "Jon, you are our leader. God has placed you here. We respect you and wherever you go, we'll follow." It blew me away.

This man saw me as a leader, and so does God. For you to stop looking at the roadblocks and to step out and lead, you simply have to change the way you view yourself. The most powerful way to change that is to believe God's Word and build your foundation for leadership upon His promises. God promised this to Joshua in Joshua 1:5-6, "As I was with Moses, so I will be with you; I will never leave you nor forsake you. Be strong and courageous, because you will lead these people to inherit the land I swore to their forefathers to give them." God's promise for you is the same.

For those of you whose insecurities are grounded in what others think of you, take on the marching orders of Timothy, a young pastor. Paul exhorted him in 1 Timothy 4:12, "Don't let anyone look down on you because you are young, but set an example for the believers in speech, in life, in love, in faith and in purity." Timothy was probably experiencing some backlash from those he was leading, and the obvious reason was his age. Leaders experience backlash from time to time. If your difficulty is due to your character traits, you had better ask God to help you change your heart. If it is because of your age, experience, or circumstances you cannot control; then take this verse to heart. Paul believed in Timothy, and God believes in you.

It is time to stop believing the misinformation and start leading. You are the right leader in the right place at the right time. God did not have a mental slip when He placed you in leadership. He knew exactly what He was doing. Your job, through the power of the Holy Spirit, is to prove Him right.

Chapter 2:
Self-Leadership
Spencer Click

Leadership is a broad topic—there are literally hundreds of different ways to write about it. A quick search on Amazon™ produces over 60,000 options for books on leadership, and I have read dozens while trying to improve my skills. Many of these are great books and can help you improve your abilities...for a season. But without doing the heavy lifting first, no matter how many books you read or how many seminars you attend, you won't maintain long-term improvement in your leadership level:

> Everyone who hears these words of mine and puts them into practice is like a wise man who built his house on the rock. The rain came down, the streams rose, and the winds blew and beat against that house; yet it did not fall, because it had its foundation on the rock. But everyone who hears these words of mine and does not put them into practice is like a foolish man who built his house on sand. The rain came down, the streams rose, and the winds blew and beat against that house, and it fell with a great crash.
> Matthew 7:24-27

Foundations are laid from the bottom up; once something is built, obviously you can't go back to the beginning and start over. So it's easier to fix the plans for a foundation, as opposed to fixing something that is already built. But by making improvements to the fundamental building blocks, big changes can be seen. You are who you are—your life, family, and experiences have formed you—but that doesn't mean you can't change: "You have taken off your old self with its practices and have put on the new self, which is being renewed in knowledge in the image of its Creator" (Col. 3:9,10). This verse doesn't just apply to your spirit; it applies to all of you. You have been made new in entirety.

It is easy to view things as being spiritual or not spiritual, but the reality is everything is spiritual. Your emotions, your heart, your mind, and your leadership are all tied together. When you start looking at your leadership as a spiritual part of life, you can really start to dig into what needs to grow and change in order for you to become the leader God has called you to be. God wants more for you. He wants you to be an amazing leader. And you can be an amazing leader—it may just take some time. You must first learn to strip away the old leader so you can lay the correct foundation for the new leader.

Second Peter speaks well to the topic of self-leadership. God has given us all we need to be successful, so we must continually add to what He has given us in order to see growth and success:

> His divine power has given us everything we need for a life and godliness through our knowledge of him who called us by his own glory and goodness…For this very reason, make every effort to add to your faith goodness; and to goodness, knowledge; and to knowledge, self-control; and to self-control, perseverance; and to perseverance, godliness; and to godliness, brotherly kindness; and to brotherly kindness, love. For if you possess these qualities in increasing measure, they will keep you from being ineffective and unproductive in your knowledge of our Lord Jesus Christ…For if you do these things, you will never fall, and you will receive a rich welcome into the eternal kingdom of our Lord and Savior Jesus Christ.
>
> 2 Peter 1:3-11

Have you ever blown up at a volunteer? Been brought to tears by a leader who snaps at you? Are you afraid of confrontation? Do you dread asking someone to volunteer because he/she may say no? My guess is there has been something in your past that has caused you to react and behave the way you do. As George Santayana says, "Those who cannot remember the past are condemned to repeat it."

I've served at several churches, and I've had varying amounts of success at the churches where I've ministered. As I've talked to friends and mentors in my life, I have found patterns in my experiences. The problems were the same from church to church. Some problems are universal to churches, but other problems were unique to me. As it turns out, I was the main problem.

One of the most mature statements I have ever heard was from a volunteer who was talking about dealing with problems in life. She was having a rough time at work, in her marriage, and pretty much everywhere else. As she was talking to me, she was seriously considering moving as a means to get away from her problems; but then she stopped and asked, "What if I am the problem?"

Do you keep running into the same problems wherever you go? It's doubtful the problems are waiting for you to show up. More than likely, you bring them with you. That's why no leadership book will ever improve things for you long term if you don't deal with the root issue that is hindering you. Inevitably you will always come back to your original problem.

Earlier I referred to "the heavy lifting"; now, let me define it. Heavy lifting is fixing the foundation that is causing the house to sag. It's not the easiest thing to do—if it were, then there would be no people with issues. If it were easy, then there would not be whole industries dedicated to self-improvement and mental health. Not every issue needs a psychologist and counseling (some do), but oftentimes just looking at why you do what you do and getting an outside perspective can help you locate blind spots in your life and leadership style.

There are many great tools to help you define your personality or leadership style: books, personality profiles, and leadership assessments are great ways to learn about yourself. Over the years, I have taken several personality profile tests—Myers-Briggs™, Strength-Finder™, DISC™, and PEP™—I even took one that classified people as lions, otters, retrievers, or beavers. All of these were good tests for identifying who I am as a person. They showed me my strengths, and they pointed out weaknesses of my personality type. They reinforced what I already knew about myself: I am a dominant personality that can sometimes overwhelm people—no surprise to anyone who knows me.

If you have taken a personality test, but didn't really dig in to the results, then you missed the purpose of the test. For me, it wasn't until I took a personality test and went through it with a fine-tooth comb that I found the true strengths and weaknesses of my personality—but I didn't initiate the digging on my own. It was done with a team of people who were also growing as leaders.

It was done with a mentor who was also growing as a leader. It wasn't done in a vacuum—the key to me moving beyond my tendencies and coming into a new place of leadership. I had people around me who pointed out when I did something that needed to be improved on. I wasn't relying strictly on myself to learn how to be better.

I decided I was tired of facing the same problems over and over. So I sought out mentors. I looked for people who had something to teach. They weren't just people in children's ministry—one of my mentors has never worked a day of his life as a children's pastor, but he has been one of the best influencers in my life and has helped me grow well beyond what I could have done on my own.

Mentors and peers have been absolutely vital to my learning how to lead myself. Self-leadership doesn't mean figuring it out all alone—it means figuring out what it takes to move you forward. Planes have autopilot, but they can't repair themselves. You also need help. Quit trying to walk through everything by yourself. Find mentor or peer groups that will help you do some heavy lifting.

As a leader, you lead people. Sometimes you don't lead people the way you think you do. It's like a play: every play has four interpretations: the writer's, the director's, the actor's, and the audience's. Your leadership is the same. When you say something, you mean it one way, but your volunteer interprets it differently. Was the volunteer wrong? Maybe. But maybe you didn't say what you thought you said.

I have a tendency to use wit, often referred to as sarcasm, a lot. My wife and I have an understanding: I don't pick on her, and if I say something that can be taken two ways, I meant it the good way. Your volunteers might give you that same leeway, but then again they might not. The only way to find out is to ask them. A great way to find out how you are leading your volunteers is to use a 360-degree evaluation. A 360-degree evaluation is when you allow those you lead to give you feedback as to how you are doing. For this to be an effective tool, you must be willing to hear something about yourself that you might not like. You must also choose wisely who evaluates you: don't pick your biggest fan; likewise, don't pick your biggest detractor. Find a balance.

After each meeting, I ask a few volunteers if I was clear, if I needed to do anything differently, if I responded poorly to someone, and what their overall impressions of the meeting were. I have some volunteers who are willing to let me know when I need to make changes, and I do my best to listen to them. It has helped me to make sure I don't repeat the same mistakes over and over. There are plenty of new mistakes for me to make.

Find some folks in your ministry that support the ministry and are willing to speak lovingly and honestly into your leadership life, and then make the adjustments needed to grow.

The journey of self-leadership is not an easy one. It takes time, it takes evaluation, and it takes change. That's the hardest part—change. Managing change is hard because without constant checking in and evaluation, *you will go back to what you've always done before*. It's just that simple.

If you don't keep change in the forefront of your thoughts and continually evaluate where you need to grow, you will not continue growing. Our history and habits are like a La-Z-Boy™ recliner—we like them and they're comfortable, so they are so easy to return to.

Change is also made difficult because people you have known for years will not believe it to be genuine—they might see it as a temporary thing. This is especially true with volunteers you may have hurt or disappointed over the years. The best way to deal with it is straight on. Apologize and ask for forgiveness where appropriate, and then show people the change by being a different leader.

Your self-leadership journey will never be over. You will not hit a place where you've "arrived." When you start looking for the place of arrival, look around; you're probably sitting on a plateau in you development. The journey to self-leadership is worth it. It is how you lay the foundation for all the other leadership areas in your life. Lead yourself well, and others will follow. Lead yourself well and you will grow. Lead yourself well and become the amazing leader has called you to be.

Chapter 3:
Living by Priorities: Getting Off the Wheel
Lisa Walker

You know the moment. You have run all week with church meetings, ball practices, work, etc., and you have decided that since it is Saturday, you are not going to do one thing but lie around the house. Forget the fact that your home is wrecked, and the health department would condemn it if they knew.

But then the phone rings. It's your in-laws who are stopping by in half an hour for a surprise visit. Time is now of the essence, and all of the sudden your entire family becomes the record-breaking-Olympic-gold-medalists-house-cleaning team! (Or you threaten to beat them, right?)

Time seems to be the one thing that no one has enough of, and unfortunately, many people operate in flight-or-fight circumstances most weeks as children's ministry leaders as well. It would seem by the way most of us act that time only matters in critical moments or when it offers immediate rewards. Often, we find ourselves running around trying to be the teacher, puppet leader, worship leader, substitute for all the volunteers who did not show, etc. The lifestyle of trying to keep all of the plates spinning is exhausting to say the least, and it often leaves one feeling unfulfilled and hopeless. Even though we seem to make it all work when we have to, running on this hamster wheel allows no time to pull together even twenty minutes of productivity.

What if there were a better way?

The most valuable leadership principle I have learned is to live by priorities. Although many folks struggle in this area, it is a principle that can change your life if you allow it. It will bring balance to your ministry, maximize how you use your time, and move you to the next level of leadership.

Unfortunately, time is fixed. We can't add one minute to the 1,440 that God gives each day. It is the one resource that we can't get more of. So it is imperative that we learn to make the most of what we have. We may not be able to manage time itself, but we can control and manage what thoughts and activities we allow to fill it by establishing and living by priorities.

Philippians 4:13 assures that we can do "all things through Christ" who gives us strength. The question is do you want to get off of the wheel and make the necessary changes in your life? God never intended for us to run tirelessly without vision. In fact, Scripture declares that with no vision, people will perish (Prov. 29:18). God wants for us to have life in abundance with vision and purpose. The most important plans for our lives cannot be determined or set by other individuals' agendas or even our own. Only God knows what His best is for our lives and what will lead us into that abundant life He wishes for us. In order to experience this abundant life God has for us, we must first forget everyone else's agenda, including our own, and **realize God's agenda**. Secondly, we need to **discover our God-given roles** so we can establish priorities that enable us to fulfill those roles. Third, we need to **set goals** that provide direction for living out those priorities, and we should revisit those goals often to evaluate our progress and to ensure we are using our time in ways that reflect those priorities.

So, how do you **know God's agenda for your life**? Have you asked Him? Have you really gotten alone before God and surrendered your will to His desires for your life? How did Jesus spend time with God? Scripture teaches that He went out early in the morning to meet with God.

Now, I struggle here. I am NOT a morning person by any definition, but I am learning to seek God in prayer those first few minutes of each day. I also save time later in the day for study and prayer when my body is actually functioning. My time with the Lord is crucial to my spiritual journey as a believer and a leader. If Jesus needed time with His father, we need it so much more. D.L. Moody commented, "If you have so much business to attend to that you have no time to pray, depend on it, you have more business on hand than God ever intended you should have."*

If we truly want to know what God has for us, we need to spend time in prayer and in His Word. He cannot speak to us if we are not in His Word daily. Let me encourage you to make an appointment with Him every day. I know from personal experience that your time with God will get pushed back every day unless you place it on your schedule and plan for it to happen.

Secondly, we need to **understand our God-given roles and priorities**. I learned this process from Jim Wideman's book *Children's Ministry Leadership: The You-Can-Do-It Guide*. Let's take a quick look at what Brother Jim has taught me:

> Get alone and take time to identify all of your roles (e.g., mom, dad, wife, son, teacher, children's minister, etc.). There will be a lot, so be sure to write them all down. Then, go back and identify the most important ones—the ones only you can do. You really have to spend some time with God as you identify your priorities and in what order they should fall. Proverbs 14:12 says, "There is a way that seems right to man, but in the end it leads to death."

Do you remember the parable of the talents in Matthew 25:14-30? The servant who buried his money for fear of losing it not only failed to increase what he had, but he actually lost what he had been given. How devastating! When we miss God's plan for our lives, we can actually lose what has been given to us. Make sure your priorities line up with the Word of God.

Once you've identified your roles, the next step is to figure out how to fulfill that role with excellence. Begin with what God's Word says about it. Then list all of your ideas. Once finished, go back and identify what the top five are. We don't fail to do the right things intentionally. We stumble because we haven't planned. You will get busy, so know which priorities are biblical and feel confident that you are doing the right thing.

Living by priorities brings true freedom. Trying to please everyone never works. I felt guilty when I spent time with my family because I knew there was so much work left unattended. And yet when I was involved in work, I felt guilty that I was not with my family. In case you haven't heard already, allow me to share. You will never go home one day when everything in ministry will be done. So let go! You have to put the priorities into your weekly schedule first, and then schedule your other responsibilities around those. The biggest gift you can give people is to be 100 percent present with them. When you live by priorities, you don't have to feel guilty because you know everything is accounted for.

Just knowing the roles and priorities for your life isn't enough. You must keep them in front of you continually for true life change to occur. You need a roadmap to help you on your journey. **Setting goals** and evaluating them often is the roadmap that will keep you focused. I get alone with God once a year specifically for prayer and to seek His plan for me. Then I map out the goals that He has shown me, breaking them down into steps and assigning dates that move me forward. I also count on close ministry peers to hold me accountable.

One tool I have found extremely helpful is Franklin Covey's PlanPlus™, which is compatible with Microsoft Outlook™. I have all of my goals plugged in, and I am able to manage all of my work through this program. Every Sunday evening I review my goals and priorities and set my schedule for the week. By doing this, I am reminded of what's most important and am able to evaluate if my actions and time line up with my priorities. If my top priority for the week (next to time with the Lord) is my family, my schedule should reflect that. If not, there is a problem. On Sunday, I plan my work, so when I come in on Monday, I work the plan.

Evaluating daily is also very important. Early in our Infuse journey, Jim asked us to track how we actually spent our time. I quickly came to a humbling realization that a lot of how I spent my time at work had little to do with my job. Being a highly relational worker, I tend to be people oriented and not task oriented. As a result, I can easily spend an entire day at work and not get one stinking thing accomplished other than spending time with people.

Evaluating how I actually spend my time has been sobering. In his book *Getting Things Done,* David Allen predicts an average worker has approximately seventeen interactions a day. Essentially, there are only about three minutes to focus on any one thing without an interruption. Once I compared that to how I spend my time each day, I became keenly aware of the many timewasters that creep in. Knowing this will enable you to eliminate those traps, and it will free you to accomplish the things that matter most.

Leo Tolstoy said, "Everyone thinks of changing the world, but no one thinks of changing himself." But true self-evaluation and change are what push us to higher levels and greater fulfillment in God's ultimate plan for our lives.

Wise King Solomon told us to "hold on to instruction, do not let it go; guard it well, for it is your life" (Prov. 4:13).

Learning to live by priorities is now my life, and I do have to guard it, for it truly allows me to honor God in the way I spend my time and, essentially, my life. My prayer for you is that God will reveal His greater plan for your life and that He will give you the passion to embark on that journey with Him. You truly can have the abundant life. So what's holding you back? Get off the wheel and jump in.

Chapter 4:
Thinking in Steps
Sara Richards

If you would have asked me two years ago to describe how I was doing as a kids' pastor, I could have summed it up in one word, *overwhelmed*. I felt like I was always working in circles and not usually able to accomplish much. I would regularly come to my team of staff and volunteers with a huge list of ideas and goals. At first, they were as excited about the ideas as I was, but then after a while, we all would realize we weren't accomplishing much at all. I'd get frustrated because we'd only get to one or two things on our lists. I knew if I was frustrated and overwhelmed, my staff and volunteers were most likely feeling that way too and probably even more than I was. Part of the problem was that I didn't really have a plan. All those goals just sounded like good ideas, but they were really just lists with no direction.

It took me a while, but I realized I was a leader without a plan, at least not a plan that was clear and manageable. And I learned from a very wise man Jim Wideman (Bro. Jim) that people follow a person who has a plan.

When I started Infuse and heard Bro. Jim talk about breaking things down into manageable steps, I was relieved. I thought, *This is the solution to my problem.* It sounded simple enough: put my ideas into a plan—a plan with steps. But soon I realized I didn't really know what he meant by "manageable steps." How do I take my vision, big ideas, goals, or even my overwhelming challenges and turn them into steps?

It wasn't until Bro. Jim gave us the assignment in Infuse to come up with goals for ourselves and then break them into steps that I actually figured out how to do this successfully. I had no idea I could do this, and when I figured out I could do this, it changed my life. Now, on days when I start to feel overwhelmed, I stop and remember that I've done what I need to do. I have a plan in place; all I need to do is work the plan.

Obviously I'm not an expert in this, but here's the process I use to develop my plans.

1. I jot down my vision, idea, or goal; and then I talk to God about it. I want to make sure what I do lines up with what He wants me to be doing. James 4:13-15 says:

> Now listen, you who say, "Today or tomorrow we will go to this or that city, spend a year there, carry on business and make money." Why, you do not even know what will happen tomorrow. What is your life? You are a mist that appears for a little while and then vanishes. Instead, you ought to say, "If it is the Lord's will, we will live and do this or that."

We need to base our goals and plans on what God wants for us; otherwise, there really is no point in making plans.

Next, I pray Proverbs 16:3 over my vision, idea, or goal: "Commit to the Lord whatever you do, and your plans will succeed." I truly believe that I cannot do what I do without God's help, nor do I want to do anything without God's help!

2. I make a list of everything it would take to accomplish my goal, vision, or idea. This is a brainstorming session for me; I try to think of every detail, every task, everything I would need to pull my idea off. I try to keep what Jesus said in Luke 14:28-30 in mind:

> "Suppose one of you wants to build a tower. Will he not first sit down and estimate the cost to see if he has enough money to complete it? For if he lays the foundation and is not able to finish it, everyone who sees it will ridicule him, saying, 'This fellow began to build and was not able to finish.'"

If I don't do the groundwork now and figure out the details, I may not see this thing come to pass, but I want to be a finisher.

3. I organize my brainstorming list into a logical order. I begin with the things that need to get done first, and then I pray Proverbs 16:9, which says, "In his heart a man plans his course, but the Lord determines his steps." Once I have asked for the Lord's help in the process, I make sure that my steps aren't too big; Bro. Jim always says, "Take steps, not leaps." If I make a step too big in the process, then I may get overwhelmed and want to give up. Knowing whether or not the steps are too big just takes practice. If you come to a step that is too big, just break it up into steps that are smaller.

4. I give myself a due date for each step. I try to be realistic with my dates because I know other things in ministry will come up, so I need to make room for those things as well. I want to make sure I get each step accomplished when it needs to be done so I can move on to the next step. I make sure I put each step on my calendar so I know when to work on it and when it's due. Putting it on my calendar helps me remember to do each step, and it helps me keep each step prioritized in my schedule.

5. Now that I know my steps, it's time to start doing them; or as Bro Jim says, it's time to start "working the plan." As I work the plan step-by-step, I celebrate. I don't know about you, but I love to be able to check things off my to-do lists. So when I get one of my steps accomplished, it's a celebration for me. I also make sure I thank God for allowing me to get that step done, and I give Him the glory for guiding my steps.

6. Evaluate, evaluate, evaluate. This is a hard one for me because of how much I hate failing. If one of my goals gets off track, it really bugs me. I have had to work really hard on this, and I've realized I need to be more flexible. Sometimes plans will change; sometimes things will even have to be put on hold indefinitely. We all know working in ministry that things come up; there are emergencies; our pastors ask us to do unexpected tasks; and sometimes things just don't go the way we planned.

I wonder if any of the disciples got frustrated when Jesus interrupted their plans by calling them to His ministry. The Bible sure doesn't talk about it if they did. I also wondered if David was bummed that he couldn't be a shepherd anymore when Saul's servant came and got him from a field one day to be an armor bearer (little did Saul know that one day David would become king). I doubt David minded because he knew unexpected things come up, and ministry is sometimes unpredictable.

We may get frustrated if we get off track, or we may even start to lose focus. That's why it's so important to evaluate on a regular basis. I try to evaluate where I am in my plan every week or, at the very least, every other week. This helps me see what I need to readjust or revise so I can get back on course. And I have learned not to beat myself up if I have to readjust. Who knows? It might have been part of God's plan all along.

I have to admit this is a new realization for me, and I am still learning how to help my staff and volunteers use this same process. I do know that if I want to help others think in steps, I need to model the process for them. I've also found that it is important for me to communicate the plan with others so they know that there are manageable steps to fulfill in order to accomplish our goals. If I can show them the steps it will take to get our goal accomplished, then they will have confidence in the plan. They need to see the plan working step-by-step, and we all need to be able to celebrate together along the way and give God the glory when we see the vision, idea, or goal come to pass.

Now, when I present my vision, big ideas, or goals to my staff, I show them I have a plan for us to follow. I present it in a way that's doable and not out of reach; it's not an overwhelming goal or process because it's broken down into steps. It gives me confidence in myself, and it also gives my staff and volunteers more confidence in my leadership abilities.

Chapter 5:
Self-Discipline: How to Do What You Don't Want to Do
Larry Hillman

Most of us go about our daily lives following the same routine day after day getting the same results as always yet still wanting so much more. But we only get more when we make changes to that daily routine. This change is seldom easy, which is why so few people do it, and it requires self-discipline.

Plato said, "The first and best victory is to conquer self." Nations have risen and fallen; companies, marriages and churches have flourished or died; all have happened because of self-discipline or the lack thereof.

An easy definition of *self-discipline* is doing what needs to be done in the right way at the right time. When the boss is watching, most anyone will give his or her best effort. The true test of self-discipline is what you do when the boss is not watching; how clean you keep your house when no one is coming over; the way you act when no one is watching.

> Go to the ant, you sluggard;
>> consider its ways and be wise!
> It has no commander,
>> no overseer or ruler,
> yet it stores its provisions in summer
>> and gathers its food at harvest.

Proverbs 6:6-8

That is true self-discipline. The ant has no commander or ruler, and yet it does everything in the right way and at the right time. I know people like to admire the majesty of the eagle, the courage of a lion, or the strength of a bull. But we would all do better to admire the commitment, consistency, and self-discipline of the ant.

We all have tasks, jobs, or areas in our lives that we do not like to address or deal with. So, naturally, we put those areas last on our to-do lists. By the time we get around to doing them, we have usually worked ourselves into a fit worrying about them. We end up frustrated and out of time, so we try and get the job done in half the time that it needs, and inevitably things end badly. This just strengthens our reasoning for waiting until the last minute, and it causes us to dread those tasks even more.

Instead, here are some simple ideas that will help you successfully handle the tasks you don't want to deal with:

The first step is to **begin scheduling**. Proverbs 21:5 says, "The *plans* of the diligent lead to profit" (emphasis mine). It's time to change how you handle these "dreaded" areas. Since you can't get out of dealing with them, schedule them to be taken care of first. They may not be the first thing in the day, but make them the first thing you schedule (i.e., before you spend time scheduling anything else, pick out a place and time for the "dreaded" tasks and schedule them).

When you do this, it will remove the apprehension and frustration of wondering all day when you will have to address the task, and it will allow you to pick a time during the day when you are at your best and can allow for the proper amount of time needed to handle the task. Plus, it will force you to prepare properly for the task. When you do this, you will be set up for success with this task; whereas, before, you were set up for failure.

Another idea to help tackle your "dreaded" task is to **role-play**. When time allows for you to role-play the "dreaded" task, you will create an example of the best course of action to follow.

When you role-play, run the task over in your mind, and think of what the best action or response would be. Then, when it is time to do the task, just follow the script or example you have in your mind. This way you are not just impulsively handling the task, rather it's more like you are following a script much like an actor would do.

Once, as principal of a school, I had to suspend one of my high school students. I knew the parent personally, and I knew the news would not be taken gently. I really didn't want to face this parent, so I spent a few minutes in my office thinking about what the best principal in the world would do if they were in a meeting with this parent. Once I was prepared for the parent's response, I was set.

The meeting took place, and the parent acted just as I expected. But each time the parent spoke, I was able to respond with the words of the best principal in the world. I said some things that were really difficult to say, but it wasn't really me being brilliant; I was just following a script of what the best principal in the world would say. It ended up being a good meeting (if a suspension meeting can be good), and the parent and I got along fine for the rest of the year.

In order to role-play, you will need at least a few minutes to prepare. The first few times you do this, you may even need to write out your response. As you get better, you may only need to write down key words or be able to forgo writing anything at all. But in the end, you will benefit from preparation.

The last idea to help you with your "dreaded" task is to simply **do the right thing**. Ecclesiastes 9:10 instructs us, "Whatever your hand finds to do, do it with all your might." Sometimes we face situations that demand immediate action, so we don't have time to schedule it or role-play our responses. We have to act, and we have to act fast. In these situations, self-discipline is critical. Too many people when faced with a crisis respond out of fear or emotion. Self-discipline will allow you to control your fears and emotions rather than be controlled by them.

All of us have heard stories of people who have reacted emotionally or fearfully and made a bad situation worse. But that doesn't always have to be the case.

When I was working as a teacher, one day after lunch, I opened my classroom door and noticed something in the doorway. Two days earlier, one of my students had brought a snake to class, and it escaped and had been hiding in my room. The something I had noticed in my door was the snake curled up. I don't know about you, but I hate snakes (this was way before any Animal Planet™ or the Discovery™ channel ever existed and showed the so-called "good side" of snakes). I immediately looked for the student who brought the snake to school. I wanted him to come pick it up, but the snake had other ideas. It quickly began to slither toward a hiding place. It would have been gone before the student could get to it. Already, the students in my class had been sitting for the last two days with their feet in their chairs for fear of the snake, so I couldn't just stand there and let it get away.

I did the right thing and reached down and picked up the snake as I had seen others do—right behind the head. Then I called for the owner to come while the poor snake writhed in pain from my too-tight grip (I wasn't about to let it crawl on me). On the outside I was cool and calm, but on the inside I was screaming, "Are you crazy?" But I knew it was the right thing to do, and it had to be done right then.

When you do the right thing it is seldom easy and almost always lonely. Take the example of the ladies in Luke 24:1 KJV, "Now upon the first day of the week, very early in the morning, they came unto the sepulchre, bringing the spices which they had prepared, and certain others with them." These ladies went to the sepulchre out of duty to Jesus. They were in fear of their lives; they were all alone; they knew they would receive no credit or recognition for it; but they knew it was the right thing to do. Sometimes you just have to do the right thing.

The most successful way to lead change is by example. When others see you calmly going about your job while everything around seems to be falling apart, they will want to know what your secret is. At that point, you can then begin to share some of your techniques with them.

Be careful how you share as you can easily come across as a know-it-all or as someone looking down at others. This, of course, will not help you or them. One way to avoid this is to walk through the steps you took in handling one of your "dreaded" tasks. Tell them the thoughts and feeling you were experiencing at the time. Ask them to tell of a situation they were in where they experienced similar feelings. This will let them know it is normal to have such feelings; however, it's not best to base your actions simply on feelings.

Stress that it is better to decide how to respond to a situation when things are calm, not in the heat of the moment. You don't wait until the clock goes off at 6:00 A.M. to decide if you are going to the gym. Similarly, you don't wait until you are in the middle of a disagreement to decide how you are going to react. You don't wait until you are in the middle of work to decide what you will do when the phone rings or someone wants to talk or you want to get a snack. You decide what you are going to do in these situations well before they occur. Decide when you are not under peer pressure, time constraints, or emotional stress.

When the situation arrives, you simply act on what you have already decided in the calm of a clear mind. Don't stop and think about your problem and allow the pressure to get to you; just follow out your decision, period.

Finally if you are going to lead others in self-discipline, start small: "He that is faithful in that which is least is faithful also in much" (Luke 16:10 KJV). Changing habits may seem simple, but it is rarely easy. I suggest you start with a small task or just one part of a small task. Once you have led others in mastering this task, select another and continue with a bigger task each time.

There are two main reasons why most people fail to make lasting change. One reason is they do the same thing the Israelites did thousands of years ago. Remember in Numbers 13:31-33, after the spies came back from Canaan, how the Israelites without throwing one spear, drawing a single sword, or shooting a solitary arrow, just gave up and said, "We can't do it"? They didn't even try. It is one of the saddest stories in the Bible. Don't be like them. At the very least, start by just trying because getting started is half the battle.

The second reason people fail to make lasting change is they tackle the whole mountain of change at one time. After a few days or weeks of trying and failing and trying and failing and seeing no progress, they quit. Don't look at the mountain; look at the pebble. Don't try to change the mountain; just change a pebble. Change enough pebbles, and you will change the mountain.

To help others change, you need to be consistent, caring, forgiving, encouraging, and transparent. When leading others in self-discipline, the key word is *self*.

Chapter 6:
A Good Name
Kathy King

Proverbs 22:1 says, "A good name is more desirable than great riches; to be esteemed is better than silver or gold." What does that mean for a children's pastor? Does it involve changing your name to something fun so the kids will remember it (e.g., Pastor Pauley—like St. Paul but with a twist, or the Kid Meister—an expert in kids)?

No, instead, this verse is referring to keeping our reputations above reproach. Many examples of men of integrity are given in the Bible: "In the land of Uz there lived a man whose name was Job. This man was blameless and upright; he feared God and shunned evil" (Job 1:1). If we're choosing a role model, you can't get better than that (well, unless you choose Jesus, but that's a gimme).

Another Old Testament role model for us to follow is Daniel. Government officials tried to find fault with him but were unable:

> At this, the administrators and the satraps tried to find grounds for charges against Daniel in his conduct of government affairs, but they were unable to do so. They could find no corruption in him, because he was trustworthy and neither corrupt nor negligent.
> Daniel 6:4

Or what about David as described in 1 Samuel 29:6, "You have been reliable, and I would be pleased to have you serve with me in the army. From the day you came to me until now, I have found no fault in you"? Wouldn't you love for someone to describe you as faultless?

Moving on to the New Testament, there's Joseph of Arimathea, who was described in Luke 23:50 as "a good and upright man." Then there's Nathanael of whom our Lord said, "Here is a true Israelite, in whom there is nothing false" (John 1:47).

From all these examples, it is easy to deduce that having a good reputation, character, and integrity is important to God. But how does that play out in our everyday lives? What does that mean to you and me?

People with integrity have unshakable character. They have our trust and respect. They also have a good reputation because they are reliable and responsible. They can talk the talk and walk the walk. The fact that they can be the same wherever they are speaks volumes of their character.

Perhaps it's because I'm getting older, but I'm not as concerned about whether or not I'm dressed in the latest fashion trend, attending the social event of the season, or using the latest and greatest gadgets to prove my popularity. But to some, these things have become so important that they are willing to do whatever it takes to be "with it."

Don't get me wrong; I think it's important to remain fashionable and look the best you can so you can relate to others. Likewise, you will have to keep up-to-date on technology, movies, TV programs, etc., so you can converse with your congregation on their levels. However, you have to be genuine in your walk so that folks can know you are real. They have to know that you're not behaving one way in front of your congregation and another when you think they're not around.

When people act differently at church than they do out in public, there are bound to be lapses in their behavior. Dr. Stephen R. Covey, noted business leader of today, relates how important this aspect is to the world of work, "In the last analysis, what we are communicates far more eloquently than anything we say or do."

If this current voice isn't enough, we can also look to Scripture as a guide. First Timothy 3:7 says, "He [an overseer] must also have a good reputation with outsiders, so that he will not fall into disgrace and into the devil's trap." Don't even get me started on how it affects families when the children see their ministerial parents behaving one way at church and another at home! I've seen MKs (minister's kids) totally turn from their religious upbringing because of the incongruity of their parents' lives between home and the church. What a sad commentary of lives supposedly dedicated to the Lord.

How about your life? Do you order water when you go out to eat but then refill the cup with Sprite™ when nobody is looking? Have you purchased items with the church's credit card and then kept them for yourself? Are you giving the church the number of hours they expect for your pay? Do you fudge on the number of children in your ministry so you look better in the eyes of the elders or deacons? Unfortunately, I've known ministers who think nothing of these acts and more. Jesus so vividly points out in Luke 16:11 the results of being untrustworthy, "So if you have not been trustworthy in handling worldly wealth, who will trust you with true riches?"

Honesty is an area where nowadays so many are having issues. But the good thing about being honest is you never have to remember which story to tell—you just tell the truth. It's amazing how freeing that simple feat can be.

A simple way to work on your integrity can be summed up with three *R*'s: respect for yourself, respect for others, and responsibility for what you do. Self-respect comes when you are happy with who you are, so you are free to follow your beliefs and accept your own limits. When you are able to accept yourself, you can more easily accept others and respect them. When you aren't afraid of ridicule from others, you can do what is right.

In the area of respecting others, you shouldn't just "put in your time" at the church; instead, you should cheerfully carry out your responsibilities. Respect your boss and your congregation. You won't abuse your privileges when you are respectful of your employer (the church). You respect them by how you talk about them to others. You do your job well because of your love for the Lord and because it's your responsibility as the children's pastor.

Unfortunately, the quality of integrity isn't innate, but rather it is a learned trait. Hopefully, this process of character development began when you were young, and you observed the examples of your family, friends, teachers, and other role models. The process was then increased by what you read or viewed or heard as you grew older. But, even if you happen to come from a less-than-perfect background, there's hope. By making a conscious effort now, you can correct your background.

The answer to developing a life of integrity is easy. It's a matter of a change of heart. Your heart has to want to change, to give Christ full control of your every move. To do that, you must seek the Lord daily, immersing yourself in

His Word so that through Him, your desires become His. Knowing how is easy, but actually following through with this daily commitment isn't.

And, this change won't take place overnight. It's a step-by-step process that you can develop. You must practice integrity in each and every thing you do so that it becomes second nature to you. If your every act speaks of integrity, then you will develop a habit of integrity. And habits become a way of life.

Since ministries tend to take on the personality of their leadership, leading with integrity means having a ministry with integrity. People who have integrity will naturally want to be a part of your team when you lead with integrity. They will be drawn to you because of your like values.

If a breach of integrity does occur, though, you must admit your mistake and take responsibility for your actions. Gen. Robert E. Lee at Gettysburg is a clear example of this when he took ownership after Pickett's charge where the army was defeated. Lee told his men, "All this has been my fault. It is I who have lost the fight." When the men heard Gen. Lee's admittance, they claimed ownership and begged to be allowed to attack the enemy again. When leaders exemplify integrity and character by admitting when they are wrong, amazing things can happen as their followers tend to trust them more and will follow them anywhere.

Learning integrity isn't something you can get from a book or course, but you can benefit from studying examples and role models from the Bible and history. Observe how their values are played out in their everyday lives, and apply those principles to your own situations. You can also learn from their mistakes, and try not to make the same ones in your own life.

Another option is to find someone whose character you admire, and ask that person to coach or mentor you. Study their values. Listen to their views. With their permission, talk with their staff and learn about their relationships. Learn how they work together, and try to duplicate those actions within your own setting. Find out how your coach or mentor deals with the pressures of life, how he or she determines what's right and wrong. Then, back that up with your own search of the Scriptures to see that the principles are biblical.

After all the studying, the next step is to get feedback from those whom you lead. Develop a climate where it's acceptable to be open and honest with each other. Engage your workers in discussions about how they feel about the issues that affect them. Talk about integrity in general. Find out if it's important to them. See what their perceptions of you are. Maybe your walk isn't so clear. Be prepared to change as needed.

Joshua 1:9 tells us to have courage, "Have I not commanded you? Be strong and courageous. Do not be terrified; do not be discouraged, for the Lord your God will be with you wherever you go." Integrity takes courage. It takes strength. But we have the power to stand up to the challenge. We can do it with His help.

Chapter 7:
Vision
Lisa Walker

This week I had my yearly eye exam, so naturally I began to wonder just how much my vision has changed over this past year. I definitely know there have been changes. It seemed to happen almost overnight. I tried blaming new medications, illness, and then the reality began to set in that I had officially crossed over the threshold into my forties. I literally thought someone had stolen all of my Bibles and books and changed the fonts in them as some kind of sadistic joke. I can assure you, I'm not finding it very amusing. For heaven's sake, I absolutely refuse to purchase, let alone wear, a pair of reading glasses as long as I have one good arm to hold out my reading material.

Some people have great vision naturally. An optometrist's diagnosis would be 20/20 or perfect vision. Others, like me, need corrective lenses in order to see properly. As I thought about my actual physical eye exam, the Lord spoke to my spirit about the spiritual aspects of vision. Two of the most important things I have learned in leadership are the importance of having a God-given vision for my ministry and the value of effectively communicating that vision to the people God has placed around me.

So what are we actually talking about when we discuss the word *vision* and its implications on leadership? Vision is the power of seeing and the ability to perceive or foresee something. In other words, people of vision are empowered with the ability to see the big picture and the overall direction of where the bus is headed. Great leaders are able to master the process of communicating vision well to the people around them. We recognize the importance of vision in Proverbs 29 and that without it the people will perish. (v. 18.) In Habakkuk 2:2 we learn that we are to communicate that vision by writing it and making it clear for all to see and understand.

The first thing I do before going to God for the vision of my particular ministry is spend time with my senior pastor to learn what vision God has laid upon his heart for our church. It is imperative that your vision and the vision that God has given to your senior pastor are in agreement with one another. Amos 3:3 tells us that unless two be in agreement, they cannot walk together. God does not call us to discern what that vision is for the church. That is between your senior pastor and Him. He does, however, expect us to align our vision with that of the house.

Once, I feel pretty sure of my pastor's heart and vision, I go before God and ask Him for clear direction for how the children's ministry is to incorporate into the big picture for our church. James 1:5 tells us that if any man lacks wisdom, He is to ask God who gives freely. So, I do just that. I ask, and then I listen for Him to speak. Scripture also teaches us in Deuteronomy 4:29 that when we seek Him with our whole heart, He *will* be found. God may choose to give you the entire picture all at once, or He may reveal the process in stages. But we can be assured that if we spend time with Him on a daily basis, He will reveal Himself to us so that we can know Him better. As we come to understand and know the character of God better, we will recognize His voice and leading.

Once I know where God is leading the children's ministry, I begin to unpack and communicate that vision for the people who serve alongside of me in ministry, beginning first with my pastor. I share what I feel God has revealed, and I simply ask his opinion of whether or not he believes it fits the overall vision of the church. That way, if there is any confusion at all, details can be clarified *before* I have launched any communication to team members. After clarification from my pastor, I share that vision first with the other members of the staff so that they can see where the children's ministry's objectives fit within the overarching vision of the church. Second, I cast that vision and direction with my leadership team that is comprised of all the various children's ministries' directors. Our team follows up on a yearly basis communicating the vision and direction to everyone in our ministry who serves children and their families.

I truly believe that often we are the reason folks miss the big picture because we only communicate the *what* of our activities and we neglect the *why*. When values are clear, decisions are easy. If people can grasp the *why* of our vision, it empowers them to take ownership of the *what* and the *how*.

People really want to be a part of something exciting or bigger than themselves. Recent statistics show that volunteerism is up in America, so why do we not see the effects of that in the local church? Often, it is a direct result of individuals not having a true understanding of the *why* of the vision…if vision is communicated at all. People want to know what they are signing up for, and when they understand the importance of the *why* and can also see where the bus is headed, they begin to take ownership and use their unique giftings to fill in the gaps within the big picture.

Once you know the direction God has created for you, say it often, and put the principles where everyone can see them. There should not be anyone serving on your team who cannot communicate who you are as a ministry, what values you believe, and where you are going. If we, as leaders, do a good job keeping that vision consistently before our leaders, everyone will always know the answers to those questions. I believe things are caught as much as, if not more than, taught. As you continually communicate what God has for your ministry, you will be amazed at how it just naturally becomes a part of who everyone is.

In order to lead change within myself concerning vision, I continually evaluate if our activities line up with what we say is important in our vision. Once a year, I plan a retreat with my leadership team. I meet with my pastor prior to that retreat to make sure I am aware of any changes in his heart concerning the overall vision of the church. During this retreat, we evaluate how we did the previous year with the plans and goals that we had established, and we determine what changes need to be made to make us more effective at fulfilling God's vision for the upcoming year.

Over the past eight years in ministry, I have also discovered that skills I have learned through coaching certification are powerful tools in communicating vision. Leading through coaching allows individuals to discover for themselves the things that they didn't know that they actually knew. This process increases the probability from about 20 percent to 80 percent of them following through with what they learn or discover. That's encouraging in and of itself, but watching it take place with your team is exciting.

I recently led a children's conference for a church, and after one hour of telling them things that they wanted to learn, the Holy Spirit directed us to focus on a particular comment someone made. After asking their permission to ask some difficult questions, something amazing began to happen. Within the next few hours, they began to say and identify things they believed about kids and ministry that they didn't even realize they knew: they were not living up to the potential that God had for the children's ministry; and they identified five immediate action steps they needed to take in the next thirty days.

As the synergy in the room began to catch, these people, who thought they didn't know anything about children's ministry, were developing plans and steps that would move them closer to fulfilling their potential for the kingdom. It was also funny how after only one day together, they were repeating the "we believes" I habitually share with my own team.

Just as our physical vision varies from individual to individual, so does our spiritual vision. Some people will be able to see exactly where it is that God is leading. These folks will jump right on the bus and be ready for the ride. Others may need assistance (i.e., corrective lenses). It could be that they don't understand the *why*. It could be that the concept is a new perspective, and change could be more difficult for them. They could need more love, care, and explanation before they are ready to get on the bus. It could also be that they don't agree with or even like the vision very much. For these people, corrective lenses may not be enough. We continue to love these people because they matter to God and Scripture demands it, but they may have to actually go through surgery and be removed from your ministry area. They may need to get off the bus completely. That choice doesn't make them or you a bad person just because there is a difference in opinion. It's simply not a healthy match anymore, and in order to serve together, there has to be agreement.

All of the muscles and functions of the various parts of the eye must work together in order for a person to have the power to see. The same is true in ministry. All parts work together to produce a healthy overall ministry.

So how is your vision? What would your optometrist say about your area of ministry? Which one of these three groups of people in ministry are you? 1) The people who receive the vision from God for their ministry and are gifted naturally to communicate and put into place what the Lord has shown them. 2) The folks that may actually have a vision but are at a loss as to how to communicate that vision to others. 3) The individuals who really have no vision at all.

Do you recognize yourself in one of these three categories? When my vision is not 20/20, I know I need to make an appointment with the Optometrist. Sometimes I just need a correction in my lenses or a fresh perspective of things. Other times I need some surgery performed in order to see clearly.

When our vision is healthy and we communicate it often and clearly to those serving beside us, we can see great things happen. Leadership can be summed up in one word—*influence*. If you look around and no one is following you, you are not leading; you are just taking a walk. People want to follow people who have vision and direction for their lives and ministries.

Chapter 8:
Don't Do It Alone: Build a Team
Jenny Funderburke

It was the perfect volunteer storm. It was July 4th weekend, so a number of volunteers were vacationing. On top of that, a summer stomach illness was circulating. Our substitutes were out. Our substitutes' substitutes were out. We had made all the calls we could, and then we went into the morning with a little fear and trembling. We were a skeleton crew, and, of course, the children were there in droves. That morning, I was worship leader, I taught children's worship, I was the greeter, and I taught a second grade small group. It was one of those mornings when I went home exhausted and frustrated. But then I heard God whisper in my ear, "That is exactly why I don't call you to do ministry alone."

You aren't called to do ministry alone either. Too often in children's ministry we get caught up in a Lone-Ranger-type mentality. But that is not how God designed ministry. Ephesians 4:11-12 says that God created leaders of the church "to prepare God's people for works of service, so that the body of Christ may be built up." Our job is to equip the people of our congregation to do children's ministry, not to do it all by ourselves. Whether you are in a church of thousands or a church of dozens, God's calling is for you to do ministry life-on-life with other people.

Isn't that exactly what Jesus did? He spent the three years of His earthly ministry pouring into His disciples. He taught them, He trained them, and He sent them out to do His work. He was the Son of God, yet He chose not to do ministry alone, so why do we? One of the most valuable leadership lessons I have learned is to build and invest in a team of people. This is essential in children's ministry for several reasons. First, as we read in Ephesians, this is what we're called to do. God expects us to prepare others to do His work. If I am the only teacher, the only decision maker, the only chair-setter-outer, the only _____ (fill in the blank with what *you* are doing), etc., I am keeping someone else from serving God. I believe He will hold me accountable for that.

Second, God can multiply the effectiveness of my ministry when I build a team. Ecclesiastes 4:9 says, "Two are better than one, because they have a good return for their work." I only have twenty-four hours in my day. When I have a team who can help me accomplish the tasks of ministry, I am free to do other things that God has set out for me to do. If I'm not the one checking in kids, I am free to have a conversation with the mama who is going through a divorce. If I'm not the one teaching in large group time, I am free to walk through other areas of the ministry to affirm volunteers and to see what needs to be improved in our systems.

Third, sharing ministry with others is a lot more fun than trying to do it by myself. When you have a team, you have someone with whom you can celebrate the wins, share the frustrations, brainstorm the challenges, and laugh over the goofy things that happen.

The first step in building a team is determining what you need. You need to make a list. Make a list of every task that you are responsible for—large and small. Now, choose a way to prioritize (by importance, by the amount of time the tasks take, or even by the tasks you love and hate). Read through your list again, and identify what someone else could do.

Here's a different way I think about it. If I disappeared from the planet next Sunday, what would go undone? That is the area where I am doing ministry alone, so I need to identify someone to come alongside of me. What pieces of ministry fall into this category for you? Even if the task is something you don't feel you can totally give away yet, you at least need a strong second string of leadership.

Remember, the point of this is not to free you up so that you can have lazy Sundays. No, the point is to empower you to do more. You can dream bigger, cast vision better, and use time more wisely when you are not the one refilling the baby wipes. Additionally, you are not identifying items that you are "too good" to do. You must be willing to do anything that must be done. That is part of ministry. But any system that depends on you and you alone is unhealthy.

You can't build a team in a day, but you can start small. Start by giving away small tasks or identifying one program that you can give more and more ownership to a key volunteer. If you are truly in a situation where you are a one-man or one-woman show, start by just finding a friend (other than your spouse) to do that show with you.

The great part about a team is that it reflects God's picture of the church. It is a body made up of various talents and personalities and gifts:

> "Now the body is not made up of one part but of many.
> "In fact God has arranged the parts in the body, every one of them, just as he wanted them to be"
> 1 Cor. 12:14,18

Your job as the leader of this ministry is to identify what the structure of this body needs to be in order to get the right parts serving in the right places.

Now that you have identified what you can empower others to do, the next step is identifying the people who are going to fill your team. I don't know about your church, but I don't have a line of people begging for more responsibility. More importantly, I don't just want people—I want the right people.

The key is to ask the Lord to show you the right people. This should be a no-brainer for those of us in ministry, but I know I have to be reminded frequently. God knows my needs. It is His plan to use the people of His church to accomplish His work. Philippians 4:19 says, "My God will meet all your needs according to his glorious riches in Christ Jesus." Yet how quickly we forget that this applies to our volunteer needs in ministry.

The higher the level of leader you are trying to find, the more selective you need to be. I handpick my leaders. I want the very best. I don't want someone who will do it because no one else will, or someone who is interested for the wrong reasons. I look for those volunteers who are committed, dependable, have caught the heartbeat of the ministry, can solve problems by themselves, and most of all are enjoyable to spend time with.

While formal training, job descriptions, policies, and such are extremely important, I have found the best way I can build a team is to simply live life with them. Jesus lived life with His disciples, and He intentionally invested even more in Peter, James, and John. I must be just as intentional in investing in my highest levels of leadership. I affectionately refer to them as my "BFFs".

They are the ones I talk to while I am driving. If a text comes in, it is likely from one of them. They know my family and I know theirs. We are doing life together while we do the work of the ministry.

Out of this relationship come the training and the impartation of leadership skills. Identify what you want these leaders to do and how you want them to do it. Model how you want them to do ministry. Communicate your expectations clearly, and communicate both encouragement and kind correction. Give ownership along with responsibility. All of these tasks are challenging, but they are made a hundred times easier when based on the foundation of relationship.

Many churches are used to a children's minister who does it all. Transitioning to a team approach, particularly to one that doesn't make you the star of the show anymore, can be quite a change in perception. Many may feel you are paid to "take care of those kids" and may be confused when they see you aren't the one on the stage or, *gasp,* you are sitting in big church like a normal person.

First, recognize that this is a change in thinking for a lot of people. Be patient with them. Do not be defensive. James 1:19 reminds us, "Be quick to listen, slow to speak and slow to become angry." Allow the growth and improvements in the ministry to speak for themselves.

Be a hard worker who people enjoy being around. Both of these characteristics are critical. Good leaders are drawn to other leaders who work hard. They want to join in with you and even relieve some of your burden. At the same time, no one wants to invest precious time and energy into ministering with someone who is grumpy, standoffish, or difficult to relate to.

This is likely a transition in thinking for you too. It is easy to give away the jobs you dislike, but it can become challenging to begin to train others to multiply the jobs you love. My two passions over the past several years have been teaching our elementary kids in a large, group worship setting and organizing our unique, small-group ministry. As we've grown, those have been the two most difficult ministries to put into the hands of other people. But at the same time, those ministries are better now because they have people who can focus on them. My attention was divided, and theirs are not.

It is difficult to admit that someone else can do the ministry that you do. I have discovered that with me this can be a pride issue. It is prideful to think I am the only one that can do an aspect of the ministry well. It is prideful to have a need to be the one on center stage. Proverbs 11:2 says, "When pride comes, then comes disgrace, but with humility comes wisdom." One of the greatest mindset challenges in this process is to choose humility and wisdom.

Another way your own thinking must transition is recognizing that the more time you are investing in your team, the less time you will be personally investing in the kids of your ministry. That is hard because as children's ministers we are wired to enjoy kids a whole lot more than we love grown-ups. However, you are also wired to seek the very best for the kids in your ministry. Because your team will be investing in them as well, those kids are going to receive higher quality ministry than if you were doing it alone. Again, your ministry is being multiplied, even if you aren't the one who gets every sick-dog prayer request or every hand-drawn valentine.

I am so thankful that God has not called us to do children's ministry alone. Yes, building a team is hard work. Yes, it is a significant investment of time, energy, and emotion. And, yes, there will be days you wonder if it would not just be easier to do it by yourself. But be encouraged that by building a team, you are truly fulfilling God's calling. You are equipping His people to share the love of Jesus with His kids and to accomplish more in your church's ministry than you ever could alone. Begin praying now that the Lord will guide you as you build your team and as Ephesians 3:20 says, you will see Him "do immeasurably more than all we ask or imagine."

Chapter 9:
Love: It's the Reason We Live
Sean Reece

When you hear people talk about leadership skills, many things may come to mind: organizational skills, vision casting, motivation, recruitment, passion, or many others. And while these are all strong components of good leaders, the most important quality that we all need to have is love.

Now, I can just imagine you sitting there thinking, *Oh boy, another love crusade*. But let me share with you why I believe this is a core foundation, not just another piece of the pie and not just for children's ministry leaders or any other leadership position. It is, in fact, for all of us regardless of our profession or place in life.

Sometimes in ministry, or in anything you do repeatedly, you can lose the passion or motivation of what you're doing. That's even true in marriage. There was an old joke going around where a wife was beginning to worry about her husband's love for her. One day she finally asked her husband if he still loved her. He simply replied, "Did I tell you I love you the day we got married?" "Yes," she said. "Well, if I change my mind, I'll let you know," he said.

Sometimes we all can get in a rut by doing the same thing over and over, whether it's curriculum, programs, or training lessons. How often do we do these things without ever looking to see what new things, ideas, or strategies are out there? Even if something is working, it doesn't hurt to ask how it could be improved. And love is anything but routine: it's fresh, alive, spontaneous, and genuine.

The Bible is God's love letter to us. It's filled with story after story of God's great love for His people, followed by God's commands for us to love each other. Do you think it's just a coincidence? Probably not. So why am I on a "love crusade"? Well, first of all because God commands it. It's not a suggestion or just a good idea; it's a command.

"I give you a new commandment—to love one another. Just as I have loved you, you also are to love one another."
John 13:34

"Dear friends, if God so loved us, then we also ought to love one another."
1 John 4:11

"My commandment is this—to love one another just as I have loved you."
John 15:17

The next reason is because love is the key to living. Love transcends all boundaries. Speaking specifically to children's ministry, it doesn't matter how big or small your church body is, what your budget is like, or where you are worshiping. If you don't have love, you don't have much. You can have all of the bells and whistles, the coolest technology, and such; but the surface-coolness factor will be short lived and without depth, which is where your love comes in. Don't get me wrong; there is a place for the cool surface stuff. It can be a great initial draw into programs and ministry, but it won't be the thing that keeps them there.

Leading in love is one of the most important things you can do. First of all, you're setting the example Jesus gave us. Secondly, when you are leading in love, people tend to relate to you in a different way. They can see your heart and know your motives are pure. When you lead out of love, you are open and real to others. People like that. You might not always get full support from others, but they are much more likely to take the time to at least hear what you have to say.

Leading in love also helps in building relationships with those who serve with you. In some ways, it levels the playing field. You're not better than anyone else. You lead by serving. When others see your heart and a genuine love pouring out for those you're serving with, it makes them more comfortable and willing to be a part of a team rather than just a body filling a position or a role.

It encourages them and transforms them from fellow believers to friends and family. When you pray for them and with them, encourage them in their ministry roles, and most importantly, listen to them; it gives them a true sense of value and belonging—something we all long for.

I'm not saying you can love everyone the same. You can't. But it is still something we must do to the best of our ability. God doesn't say love is easy. Remember, He doesn't just say to love your friends but also your enemies. He knows this won't be an easy thing for us to do all of the time. This, again, is where we need Him to be pouring into our lives. The more we allow Him to do that, the more love God will give to us to flow out from us.

How this happens is very important. For us to lead in love, we must continually be connected to the One who gives us love. It is just as important for us to stay plugged into worship services, small groups, and our personal devotions. Believe me, I can tell a huge difference in my life if I miss a week or two of worship because I'm "doing ministry."

Doing ministry *never* replaces being in worship or being ministered to. Plus, your actions are the example you're setting for those you serve with. Ministry never takes the place of being connected in worship. When you volunteer in an area and use your gifts and talents, you are serving. So, first you worship and get ministered to, and then you take that and go out and use that in service for God's glory.

In regards to the children in your ministry, children are young; but they sure can pick out who is being real and who is putting on an act. They can tell when you're making small talk to act like you care about them and when you are genuinely interested in them. And this is very important because, as they are growing up and hopefully growing in Christ, they need to know that there are other adults they can feel comfortable talking with.

Kids love to talk in general. They love to tell you about their vacations, their pets, their upcoming birthday parties, and even when they win their games. But the deeper stuff they hold within can take a little longer to come out unless they trust you or another leader. Remember, building these meaningful relationships with anyone takes time. It's not a fast process, and it usually takes openness and trust.

I've heard of instances from other places in ministry where certain leaders didn't want to get too involved with certain kids because the kids were either from divorced families or already labeled as "challenging" so they might require a lot of attention. Hello? Doesn't it mention in the Bible taking care of widows and orphans? I don't think it ever gives us a time limit on loving others. Now I know we cannot pour everything out into everyone we meet, which is where it becomes important to ask God which leaders we need to be pouring into so they can multiply God's productivity in the lives of His body the church.

The relationship you create with your kids affects more than you realize. When you have a good relationship with those kids, they talk about you. They might talk about you to their parents, friends, or teachers. And the impact you have on their lives can go so much further than you realize. Think about the effect on the family you can have when little Johnny tells his mom that you prayed for him and his test this week, or when Suzie shows her dad a simple, handwritten note that says she did a great job in the Christmas play. It's the little extra things that will go a long way in growing healthy relationships, not just in your program but within the church body as well. Parents will appreciate all the extra prayer and positive encouragement for their children. Make sure you understand this: it is not about fluff or the extra icing on the cake. It's about true, heartfelt thoughtfulness that is an outpouring from being thoughtful, thinking of others before yourself, and thinking of others needs and wants before your own. These are actions that come out of who we are, not because you want to schmooze others into buying what you're selling.

Just like a stone thrown into a pond makes ripples, your love and actions can have the same effect in your church body. It can flow from the children and other leaders to the rest of the body, which can go a long way when you're recruiting new leaders. People are more likely to volunteer to serve if they perceive you as a servant leader who cares more about the people within a program than the statistics and numbers.

The same thoughts apply to the others on staff as well. When God's love flows from us, a lot of problems can be avoided. Now, remember, being full of God's love doesn't make us weak or a pushover: we try to act like Christ in all situations. Sometimes it will not be easy, especially when it comes down to program or ministry issues.

Conflicts will arise. So don't fool yourself into thinking that everything will go perfectly smooth from here on in. Just because we ask for God's love to pour into and out of us, doesn't mean we aren't are still human and sometimes make mistakes. But that is where we learn and grow. If God is going to give us more love, He is going to give us circumstances to use it.

We all know many references in the Bible that speak about how we should love and whom we should love. And a lot of times we hear the 1 Corinthians 13 passage at weddings. That passage shows us what love is to be like, not just in marriage, but in life. Love is patient, kind, does not envy, and the list goes on. Our fruit can be sweet and fragrant, or rotten and of no use. Which is more effective in ministry or in life? More importantly, which is more pleasing to God?

Simply stated in terms of what we teach our kids on a weekly basis, treat others the way you want to be treated (love); and whatever you've done for the least of these, you've done for me (we need to treat everyone as if we are doing it unto Jesus Himself).

Chapter 10:
A Servant/Leader
Larry Hillman

It seems that nowadays everyone is putting his or her two-cents worth into the discussion of how to be a good leader. There are books, seminars, and websites that list the seven ways to lead this and the five principles that can't miss on that. Many of these are very helpful, but as I began writing this chapter, I realized I didn't know what the Bible has to say about being a good leader. I did a search of the New Testament in five different translations. I first searched for *leading* and got twenty-four hits, but those were mostly about a person who was in the position of leading, not what they did as a leader. So I looked up *leader* and got fifty-four hits. Once again it was referring to an individual who had a position. Still trying to find some biblical leadership principles, I looked up *leadership*, and among all five translations of the New Testament, I got zero hits. I know there are a lot of good leadership principles in the New Testament, but there is nothing under the words I was looking for.

After thinking for a few minutes, I remembered something, so I searched for the word *servant* in the New Testament and got 209 hits! I searched for *follow* and got 246 hits! I quickly concluded that while we need great leaders, the Bible is more concerned with us being great followers. In order to be a good leader, we must first be a good follower.

While studying leadership, we have been taught that when we are the center of our life's focus, our life is selfish and has little meaning. We have been taught that if all a person is after is a title or a position, that person will not serve others. Instead, they will see themselves as positioned higher than those around them. And we know that anyone who is consumed with thoughts of their "rights" will not serve others because it is their "right" to be in charge and be served.

On the other hand, we have learned that serving others builds confidence and loyalty and involves personal sacrifice. This inspires others to follow and work harder. So in order to effectively lead others, we must serve them.

But just how do you go about being a great servant leader? Let's read what Matthew wrote:

> Then the mother of Zebedee's sons came to Jesus with her sons and, kneeling down, asked a favor of him.
>
> "What is it you want?" he asked.
>
> She said, "Grant that one of these two sons of mine may sit at your right and the other at your left in your kingdom."
>
> "You don't know what you are asking," Jesus said to them. "Can you drink the cup I am going to drink?"
>
> "We can," they answered.
>
> Jesus said to them, "You will indeed drink from my cup, but to sit at my right or left is not for me to grant. These places belong to those for whom they have been prepared by my Father."
>
> When the ten heard about this, they were indignant with the two brothers. Jesus called them together and said,
>
> "You know that the rulers of the Gentiles lord it over them, and their high officials exercise authority over them. Not so with you. Instead, whoever wants to become great among you must be your servant, and whoever wants to be first must be your slave—just as the Son of Man did not come to be served, but to serve, and to give his life as a ransom for many."
>
> Matthew 20:20-28

Did you notice Jesus did not correct James and John for wanting to have a place of prominence or leadership? Did you notice Jesus did not say it was wrong to want to be first? He didn't even correct the other disciples who upon hearing the plans of James and John began protesting that they wanted that lofty position and that they were just as deserving as James and John.

On the contrary, Jesus not only didn't correct them concerning their desires to be first, he put His approval on their desires to be first by telling them the secret to gaining that position—become the servant of others, not just to those above you but to those equal to and lower than you. The greatest disciple must serve the disciples walking right next to him. Also, remember that Jesus says it is wrong for a leader to lord power over others.

In Philippians 2:4 MSG, Paul says, "Put yourself aside, and help others get ahead. Don't be obsessed with getting your own advantage. Forget yourselves long enough to lend a helping hand." We are to think of ways to make others successful. As a leader we should do everything in our power to insure the success of those under us. As they succeed, it will increase their productivity, keep them from becoming burned out, and create a loyalty that can't be bought.

As those under you become successful, it makes you more successful and moves you further up the ladder of leadership, which is what we all want. Remember, it's not being called a leader that makes you a success, it's how you got there and what you do once you are there that determines your success.

Now that you have learned the secret of being a great leader, how do you get others to change their style and adopt this radical idea of leading by being a servant?

The answer is pretty simple. Just follow the example of the greatest leader who ever lived:

> It was just before the Passover Feast. Jesus knew that the time had come for him to leave this world and go to the Father. Having loved his own who were in the world, he now showed them the full extent of his love.
>
> The evening meal was being served, and the devil had already prompted Judas Iscariot, son of Simon, to betray Jesus. Jesus knew that the Father had put all things under his power, and that he had

come from God and was returning to God; so he got up from the meal, took off his outer clothing, and wrapped a towel around his waist. After that, he poured water into a basin and began to wash his disciples' feet, drying them with the towel that was wrapped around him.

John 13:1-5

Jesus did not teach a lesson to the disciples about being a servant; He didn't have time for that as he was about to be arrested. So to teach how to be a servant, He became one. Look at verse three; it says Jesus knew the Father had put all things under His power. Jesus knew His position, His title, and His "rights" as supreme ruler. Verse four says that because He knew this, He was able to wash their feet. The room fell silent as the disciples watched the Messiah (the One who spoke to the storm, and it obeyed Him; the One who raised Lazarus from the dead; the One whose teaching confounded the priests; the One sent from the Father) bow down and clean their toenails and wipe the dirt from between their toes.

You know, Jesus gave them the best foot washing they had ever received. He loved them too much not to do a great job of cleaning their dirty, dusty, smelly feet. And because He became their servant, the disciples loved Him more than life itself. Most, if not all, of those present in that room gave up their lives for Jesus and counted it a privilege to do so. Now, that is inspiring loyalty.

There are many ways for us to act out being a servant to others. We can stock their supplies, clean up their messes, and cover for them when they are running late. We can meet them for lunch, send birthday cards for them and their children, remember their favorite candy, and talk about their interests when we meet. Whenever we choose to go the extra mile, we will create a lasting, strong relationship, which will bear much fruit.

Matthew 20:28 says, "The Son of Man did not come to be served, but to serve, and to give his life as a ransom for many." This verse doesn't just mean that Jesus died for them, it also means He gave his life every day for them. For example, when He washed the disciples' feet, He gave up his life and took on the life of a servant. Because He became this servant, He was able to become the greatest, most inspiring leader of all time.

We, too, can become successful leaders by inspiring others to follow the example set for us by Jesus: "I have set you an example that you should do as I have done for you" (John 13:15).

Chapter 11:
Caring for Your People
Sara Richards

Two years ago, my lead pastor gave some of the staff the opportunity to meet one-on-one with an executive coach. He also gave each one of us an assignment to work on during our coaching experience. He asked me to "pastor" my volunteers.

I have to be honest and say that when I first read his assignment, I really didn't know what that meant. I thought I already was pastoring my volunteers. I was actually surprised by the assignment because I thought he would want me to focus on becoming a better recruiter.

After some clarification from him, I learned he wanted me to take the authority I'd been given to feed, guide, protect, and watch over my volunteers. *Wow*, I thought, *that sounds kind of scary*. First of all, the word *authority* hit me pretty hard. I had been given the authority to do this? I had never looked at my job in that way before. I did not feel like I was capable of doing that. Since my title was "kids' pastor," I knew how to pastor kids, but how could I pastor adults? Second, I wondered how I was going to be able to pastor 150-plus people. Even though I didn't know how, I knew I needed to try because this was an area my pastor wanted me to improve upon.

So after working with my executive coach and learning a lot from Brother Jim in Infuse, I came up with a plan and began working that plan. I determined I would protect and watch over my staff and volunteers by making sure they knew I truly cared about them. I wanted to make sure they knew our team would be a place to turn to in difficult times or in times of need. I would guide them by making sure they were on track spiritually, by giving them feedback, and by continual support from our ministry. I would feed them by teaching and providing them with resources to grow in their faith and in their service. Basically, I would truly care about each one of my volunteers.

One of the first steps in my plan was setting up a structure that would allow my staff and me to care for a reasonable number of people. I realized it is nearly impossible (and unbiblical) for me to consistently pour into and care for 150 people. Look at Exodus 18. Jethro visits Moses and discovers Moses is trying to lead the people and do everything by himself. In verses 17 and 18, Jethro tells Moses, "What you are doing is not good. You and these people who come to you will only wear yourselves out. The work is too heavy for you; you cannot handle it alone." Jethro helps Moses appoint officials over smaller groups of people so the work is manageable.

I decided it would be reasonable and manageable for me to pour into my staff of four people. I would then have my staff (directors) pour into and care for their four-to-eight coaches. My original plan was to have our coaches then pour into all the volunteers they oversee on the weekend, which could have been as many as fifteen people. However, I discovered that was too many people for the coaches to care for. Since then, we've added another level into our system and the coaches pour into and care for their room leaders, which is about four per coach. The room leaders care for and pour into the other leaders in their room.

I also suggested that each one of my staff and coaches go through our church's Life Coach training, which is training in discipleship. The training provides the leaders with resources and concrete steps on how to disciple someone one-on-one. I wanted my leaders to think of themselves as life coaches or disciplers to the people on their team.

Each of our coaches checks in with the people on his or her team on a weekly basis through emails, phone calls, and cards in the mail. Some of the people need more care than others, and some don't really need much at all; but I still want them to be available if needed.

This system also works with communication and teaching. I teach or communicate to my staff what I want the team to know, they communicate and teach it to their coaches, the coaches communicate and teach their room leaders, and so on.

Now, please don't misunderstand, this doesn't mean that I don't care directly for and communicate directly with each of my volunteers. I still make it a priority to spend time and care for them. It's important that they know me and know that I care about who they are and not just what they do in our ministry. I have made a point to learn who each one of them is and a little about their lives.

One of the ways I do this is by walking around on weekends and talking with volunteers. I do this before, after, and during the services. I ask volunteers how they are doing, and while I'm doing this, I'm gauging whether or not they are telling me what I want to hear or what is the truth. We all know there are a lot of people out there who say, "I'm okay," or "I'm alright," and they really aren't. Those words are cues for me to dig a little deeper.

I have also learned if I'm going to ask the question, I have to be willing to follow through. So if someone says they are just okay or they aren't okay, I need to take the time to find out why and find ways to help them. This is vital to showing people you really care. It's not enough to ask the question; you have to be willing to follow through. This can be simple things or things that are really tough and require a lot of time and energy.

For example, a few weeks ago one of my volunteers was having trouble watching the monthly video updates I send out via email to all our volunteers. I knew we had a guy on our Sunday morning team that works with computers for a living, so I connected the two of them and now the volunteer has no problems with his computer and watching my video updates.

Some of the more difficult ways we've needed to care for volunteers has involved helping people get connected with financial resources, or walking them through the loss of a family member or a really tough time in their lives. I usually bring other people in to help; that's what the body of Christ is for—to use our gifts to serve others. Whatever resources or people I connect the volunteer with, I always check up on the process and make sure that the volunteer is getting the help he or she needs.

Another way I care for my volunteers is by making it a priority to pray for them. When I ask for prayer requests from volunteers, I follow through by actually praying for them. I think it's become pretty easy to tell people we'll pray for them, yet then we get busy and forget to pray for them. That's why I had to come up with a way to keep track of all the prayer requests. As volunteers share requests with me on weekends, I write them in a notebook I carry with me and then later enter them into my computer. I put time into my schedule during the week to pray over the requests. I also try to follow up with them later to see how they are doing and to see how God's answered their prayers.

I now know that one of the biggest parts of my job is to take the authority I've been given and care for our volunteers, and God will help me do that. It's my mandate to care for each one of our volunteers; it's not an option. It's how the first church worked: they cared for each other's needs and didn't think twice about it. If I'm asking my volunteers to care for and serve the kids of our church, I better be willing to serve and care for our volunteers.

The best way to help others catch on to this is by modeling the things I've mentioned above. Some people just get this, and it comes naturally to them. For others it's a struggle. For those who struggle, I encourage you to not be afraid of asking more questions of people. I've instructed my staff to use their authority and push back a little bit when people say they are just "okay." They know they need to follow through as well. Additionally, if they see me following through and caring for people, they will be much more likely to follow my lead.

I also feel it's important to cast vision for the plan. When I put my plan together two years ago, I shared it with my team. I showed them the steps we would take to get this accomplished. Showing them I had a plan helped them to see we could do this together. It also showed them the things that would be required of them. Breaking our volunteers down into manageable groups allowed them to see that they could do this.

I've shared with my staff that I want our ministry to be a place where people will truly be cared for, and we will always follow through on what we say we'll do. I've told my staff that I don't ever want anyone to quit serving in kids' ministries because he/she didn't feel supported or cared for as a person. I want our ministry to be a place where people know without a doubt they are cared for. We aren't perfect, and we're still learning, but I know God will help me carry out the mandate given to me.

Chapter 12:
Managing the Chaos: Leading in Discipline and Behavior Management
Jenny Funderburke

Can you picture it? Little Johnny is under a chair while Bobby is holding one over his own head. Susie is crying because Molly said something ugly. Jimmy and Freddy are making unique noises during the lesson. Sam just kicked three kids who are smaller than him. Is that marker on the wall? And where's the adult in the room? Oh, she's there, and you're praying she comes back next week too!

We can all identify with having a Sunday (or maybe lots of Sundays) where a similar scene plays out in our children's ministry area. Behavior management is a hot topic in kids' ministry. After all, kids are kids, and their default is to push the boundaries and look for opportunities to do whatever they want to do. This results in stressed volunteers who sometimes do not want to return.

We love working with kids because of their boundless energy, creative minds, and lack of inhibitions. But those three characteristics are also what can put the best children's ministers and volunteers into early retirement. There are things that you as the leader of your ministry can do to eliminate many behavior problems and create a calmer environment for kids and volunteers.

Discipline is a word that has different connotations to different individuals. Usually people view discipline as negative, but God views it as beneficial. Proverbs 3:12 says, "The Lord disciplines those he loves"; and Proverbs 12:1 says, "Whoever loves discipline loves knowledge, but he who hates correction is stupid." When we decide that behavior management and discipline are important in our children's ministry, we are agreeing with God.

But, let's be honest, when it comes to discipline with kids, in some ways we as a church are at a disadvantage. We are not a school with a principal's office. Kids are not required by law to attend our classes, and those smart children know it. They know our consequences are limited, and they know that if they throw a big enough fit at home, they might not have to come back.

However, our advantage lies in the root of the word *discipline*–disciple. Our role is to guide these kids to be more like Christ, to become disciples. Our end goal is not silent children sitting in pristine chairs. Our goal is to help guide behavior so that our kids can become more like Jesus. Because this is our ultimate goal, effective discipline strategies should be more evident in our children's ministry than in any other environment in a kid's world.

Kids need an environment to learn about Jesus that is safe both physically and emotionally. Additionally, kids need structure so they have the maximum opportunity to learn. It is our responsibility as leaders to establish a culture in our children's ministry where our volunteers are set up for success in the area of behavior management.

The very first step in solving behavior problems is **stopping them before they happen**. Psychic abilities are not required but rather careful observation of your ministry. Identify what can be done to eliminate problems before children even walk into your building. Preparation is huge. Many classes have gone crazy while a teacher was looking for his/her supplies, so how can you simplify the process so he/she isn't hunting for crayons during class? Figure out what is happening in your physical space (too crowded? wrong-sized chairs? too many toys to play with?) that could cause issues with the children? Which distractions can be removed? Any problems you can identify and solve ahead of time will help cut down on behavior problems.

At my church, we are constantly evaluating if our curriculum and activities are age-appropriate and if they engage the kids. Bored kids quickly equal trouble. If the activities are too hard or way too easy, kids are going to come up with something else to do. If the teaching is monotone and doesn't involve them, kids aren't going to pay attention. If we are asking first graders to sit still for long periods of time, we are expecting the impossible. If we are asking fifth graders to sing songs they think are babyish, they will tune us out. It is vital that we as leaders are constantly evaluating to make sure what we are doing is meeting the needs of our kids.

We also **establish ministry-wide expectations**. We keep ours very general because making a list of 376 specific rules would result in a really long list that no one would remember. Our "Westwood Kids' Behavior Guidelines" are based off of Matthew 22:37 and 39, "Love the Lord your God with all your heart and with all your soul and with all your mind.

"Love your neighbor as yourself." Based on that, we remind our kids each week that we expect them to:

1. **Show love for God.**
2. **Show love for others.**
3. **Show love for myself.**

We often teach or give examples of how to live out those guidelines. Just about any misbehavior a kid could pull is covered by these three. We have also trained our leaders to use that same language when correcting kids and when praising kids.

In addition to ministry-wide expectations, we also have uniform ministry-wide consequences. It frustrates our volunteers when they don't know what recourse they have when a child is misbehaving. When kids misbehave, our leaders follow the following sequence:

1. **Verbal warning:** "Suzie, you aren't showing love for Tim by pulling his hair. If you don't stop, you are going to have to miss out on the fun we are having."

2. **Removal from activity:** "Suzie, you will need to sit by me for a couple of minutes while your friends are working on their art project."

3. **Removal from the room & brought to a staff member/ leadership team member.**

4. **Staff member will find parents and discuss behavior.**

We have very rarely had to find a parent during the service, but the sequence helps both parents and kids know that there is a "next step" if their behavior doesn't improve.

The goal of our ministry is to "partner with parents to help kids grow closer to Jesus." Sometimes in children's ministry we are afraid of communicating with parents about their kid's behavior. It is a fine line. We never want a parent to feel that we don't want their child to come back. Also, parents who have kids who misbehave a lot are pretty tired of hearing about their child's misbehavior. So, we must be gentle, but we must be honest too. If we are truly partnering with parents, we share the challenges as well as the joys. We ask for tips of how to best handle situations with their child. Above all, we communicate how much we love their child and how we want them to learn as much about Jesus as they can.

In order to lead change that leads to better behavior, we must first accept that this is our role as leaders of the children's ministry. While each volunteer has to be responsible for his or her individual group or class, the overall tone and culture of our ministry is our responsibility.

As the leaders of children's ministry, our job is to set our volunteers up for success in their ministries. We have to ensure that we are not creating potential for behavior problems. We have to make sure that we have enough adults in the room and that volunteers have what they need to do their jobs. We don't want our volunteers to have to deal with any behavior problems that result from things we could have prevented.

Sometimes as children's ministers we fall into the trap of wanting to be liked by everyone. Of course, we want kids to like us, but we can't let that desire override the need children have for discipline. As the lead children's minister, you may have to be the "bad guy" in some situations. Most of the time it is much better for you to be the bad guy than for the teacher or small-group leader to be in that role. We should never leave the volunteers under us feeling unsupported or like they've been hung out to dry. We need to be the ones that handle the toughest conversations and the roughest situations. The truth is we will often gain more of an audience with kids and their parents when we are willing to set boundaries. Kids innately know they need rules. When you correct them with love and with a desire to see them grow closer to Jesus, your relationship with them will be stronger. When you are honest with parents in a kind and gentle way, they know you are a true partner in helping their kids learn about Jesus.

Leading change in others in dealing with behavior management occurs predominantly through training. You want to train your volunteers thoroughly in the ministry's behavior expectations and guidelines and in what they can do within the classroom to cut down on problems. Tips such as using children's names while talking, moving closer to disruptive children, and positively reinforcing good behavior are helpful.

Equipping teachers to more effectively present their lessons could be the most beneficial behavior management training of all. Plan to train teachers to be overly prepared so the class runs smoothly and without interruption. Stress with teachers (bribe if you have to) the importance of being early so they can start the class with the right atmosphere.

You can best help make sure changes are implemented by continuously inspecting what is going on. Brag on volunteers for what they do right. Coach in areas where you see a need for improvement. Constantly keep your eyes open for ways your team can meet the needs of kids and prevent behavior issues before they start.

Some leaders may simply need to change their roles. A loud and fun college student may not be the best fit for a quieter learning environment, while a meek-mannered volunteer may not be the best fit leading crazy games. Sometimes people end up in roles that just don't fit their personalities. Kids can smell fear or inexperience, and then they may pounce. Your job is to help people find their perfect fit, which will result in less frustrated volunteers and better-behaved children.

Wouldn't it be nice if there were a magic formula for eliminating all behavior problems in children's ministry? As long as sin exists in the world, we know that can never happen. Discipline in children's ministry is not fun. But, be encouraged by Hebrews 12:11, "No discipline seems pleasant at the time, but painful. Later on, however, it produces a harvest of righteousness and peace for those who have been trained by it." What an incredible result for the children in our ministry—a harvest of righteousness and peace. That, my friends, is why we do what's hard. That's why we set expectations and have consequences. That is why we properly prepare our volunteers and coach them to get better. We do it all so our kids can experience a harvest of righteousness and peace.

What a great job we have.

Chapter 13:
Which Family Is Your Priority?
Derek Jones

Family is a word we hear and say so often in children's ministry: we want to partner with families; we have family nights, family days and family services, etc. So many times in ministry we think and talk about "the family," yet we forget our own.

Having a parent or spouse in the ministry can be the greatest blessing and the greatest curse in life. I know firsthand what it is like to grow up as a minister's kid and so does my wife. Because of our experiences growing up in ministry, it has challenged us to discuss and prepare for how we will invest in our own family.

Growing up separately, my wife and I both saw many nights at home with just our moms and sisters while our dads spent time with the church family instead of their own. My wife's mom was actually mistaken as a single parent one time when in all reality she was married to the pastor. As a child, I had to sacrifice a lot of time with my dad for the benefit of the church family. No one asked if that was okay with me. No one asked my dad if he was spending time with me before they called him to a special meeting. He was just expected to serve the church first.

From birth I was expected to know the eternal significance of my father's work and willingly sacrifice time with my dad because he was helping lead the church family. That is a lot to put on a child. It is also a lot to put on a marriage. I saw my mom work all day, take care of my sister and me, and then have some type of involvement in church activities several times per week. So, church turned into my home away from home. The church family was my family. The nursery workers rocked me, the children's leaders taught me, and the student leaders cared about me.

Looking back, I know that I had, and continue to have, amazingly supportive parents who truly love me more than anything in the world. As we were growing up, my parents would have definitely said that my sister and I were their first priority, and in their hearts we were. Their time, however, dictated differently.

They thought I was their number-one priority; and I was, no doubt, a huge priority; but the church always came first. It is really hard to argue with putting something so amazing and life changing as your highest priority, so I never did. My childhood taught me the importance of the church, and it actually taught me to value the work of the ministry.

In fact, I have followed the calling of God on my own life and now work in children's ministry. So, I have the chance to learn from the ministry choices my father made years ago. I even see my parents realizing they would change the way they prioritized family now that they are beginning to enter the grandparent stage of life. Dad calls regularly, texts all the time, and comes over to our house to fix things. We have a better relationship now than we did when I was a kid. He is the one I seek for advice and the one I call with exciting news. I know if he had things to do over again, he would choose me over the church more often.

So this brings a huge challenge to me as a minister. I believe I can accomplish more in ministry to children when I partner with their families. But if I neglect to invest in my own family by making them the priority, I have failed at the most basic calling in every minister's life. For ministers, families come first. Deuteronomy 6:5-7 says:

> Love the Lord your God with all your heart and with all your soul
> and with all your strength. These commandments that I give you
> today are to be upon your hearts. Impress them on your children.
> Talk about them when you sit at home and when you walk along
> the road, when you lie down and when you get up.

This passage is a beautiful picture of ministry. We must start by truly loving our great God with everything we are. When we keep these commands on our hearts, they will naturally pour out onto those around us. It is difficult, however, to impress the Word of God upon your children if you do not make time with them away from church a natural part of your life.

As kids' pastors, it is easy to think that the Word of God is being poured into our families because we have made the plan, designed the program, and properly executed the activities. But we have to do all the things we encourage other husbands, wives, and parents to do. I look back and see I was blessed that my dad worked with adults, so he was trading me to work with adults. Children's pastors don't have that luxury. If you don't prioritize, your kids will feel you are trading them for other kids. You are the only one who can be the mom or dad to your kids. They can have many friends, teachers, and even pastors, but you are the only one who has been given the role of parent.

Every day in ministry I am also challenged to think about the importance of investing in my relationship with my wife. This relationship can affect how I minister to kids and interact with their parents and other leaders. As I seek to find how to treat my wife and how she fits into my ministry, I am reminded of Ephesians 5:25-30:

> Husbands, love your wives, just as Christ loved the church and gave himself up for her to make her holy, cleansing her by the washing with water through the word, and to present her to himself as a radiant church, without stain or wrinkle or any other blemish, but holy and blameless. In this same way, husbands ought to love their wives as their own bodies. He who loves his wife loves himself. After all, no one ever hated his own body, but they feed and cares for their body, just as Christ does the church—for we are members of His body.

As I read these powerful words, I realize my wife is not to fit into my ministry; she is the first one I minister to. I must do my best to show her the love of Christ and to care for her as myself. We need to be spending time together in God's Word before I go out and share it with others.

We as ministry leaders with the closest relationship to families must set the example for those in our ministries by making our own families *the* priority, not just *a* priority. Like any job, ministry has busy seasons that require more of our time and attention. Keep this in mind, and plan extra time with your family before and after major events. Take a day off just for them, and skip school to simply have fun and show them they are your priority. Do whatever it takes to go with your wife on a date or to a ballgame with your husband. Maybe this means extreme planning or simple flexibility and spontaneity, but our spouses and kids must come first.

My wife knows that if she needs me, she can get to me during any meeting no matter what. Because she knows this, she truly respects my time and appointments, so she steps in only when necessary. My wife is also not the glue that holds my ministry together or the putty that fills every crack. She serves with me when she can, just like any other leader. I do not put unnecessary pressure on her to be my greatest volunteer. She is an amazing partner in ministry, and she serves with me from her strengths. We are constantly learning how to make this work, and we are fully committed to the process.

As we show the love of Christ and impress His commands onto each member of our family, the overflow of His work in their lives will spill out into the lives of those we minister to. If family is the most important influence on the lives of children, then we must be that influence on our own. We must serve our families with support, encouragement, and the sacrificial love of Christ as we faithfully serve the Lord and live out His calling on our lives. This is something we must learn and help others put into practice.

As I think about my life, my family, and the many opportunities in ministry that lie ahead of me, I do not want to look back many years down the road and see a growing church family that loves me and a family at home that I barely know. Today and every day, I must make the choice to put my family as *the* priority.

Chapter 14:
Leading in a Familiar Place
Keith Warfield

In 2005, I experienced some of the biggest changes of my life. In January, I was a single, cell-phone salesman that volunteered with the youth at my church. By August, I had been hired to assist our youth pastor, and then I led the youth group with another youth worker while our youth pastor transitioned to missions. My grandpa passed away; I got married; and while all this was going on, God was shifting my passion to children's ministry. In August, I sat before my church's deacons and elders, and I explained why I wanted to lead the children's ministry.

It was a whirlwind of a year, and I thank God I experienced it all at my home church. I love the people at my church, and I feel incredibly blessed to be able to serve with people I have known for a long time. Plus, there are a lot of people I am getting to know. No church is perfect, and each has its unique set of challenges. I have learned by talking to others and by my own mistakes that leading at the church you grew up in can have its pros and cons. It really is like working anywhere else. If you make an effort to understand your church and its people, the pros will greatly outweigh the cons.

From all the lessons I have learned, three stand out as the most important for leading at your home church. The first, **earn people's trust before making changes**. Next, **show people you can lead**. Last, **unspoken expectations will hurt you if you don't find out what they are.**

I was a volunteer with our youth ministry for three years, and I was a youth-department-staff person for five months before taking the children's minister position. When I changed jobs, I quickly realized all the time spent with the youth didn't mean much to the children's workers. They needed to know I was there and would do anything for them.

Our administrative pastor sat me down one day one and told me I would not be making any big changes in the first year. I realize now how huge that really was. It kept me out of a lot of trouble. So I spent the first year earning people's trust. I worked really hard to be dependable and try to be there to help wherever needed. I bent over backward to meet the needs of our volunteers. During the first few months, I didn't even teach. I spent most of my time observing and helping. At the time, I felt like I was not doing enough, and maybe others felt that way, but now I know that it was the best thing I could have done. It helped me understand what others needed, and it equipped me to be a better servant leader.

The first thing I did as children's pastor was pick up the phone. I called my friend Carlos who was the only children's pastor I knew. I asked him one question, "What should I do?" He told me,

"Look, bro, if there is one thing I know, it doesn't matter what you're doing, it matters what it looks like you're doing."

You have to earn people's trust no matter where you are, but at your home church you must also show them you are not the little kid image they have stuck in their minds. If you want them to think you have grown up and are responsible, you had better grow up and be responsible.

When I stepped up, I had to make some major adjustments to who I was and how I managed things. Before, I was an unorganized irresponsible mess. I didn't have a calendar, and I thought I was smart enough to keep track of everything in my head. Thankfully, soon after that I realized the best thing I could do was get a calendar and start a to-do list. My appearance was another thing I had to address. My holey jeans and "cool" t-shirts were not telling anyone I was ready to lead (how in the world our church trusted me with the children's ministry is really hard for me to imagine now). I thought I was ready for it, but the truth is I am still hard at work to be as dependable and organized as I need to be to for our church.

There are a lot of unspoken expectations you will face as you lead in a familiar environment. Some people will expect you to keep things the same because it's your church and that's how it's always been done. Unless your church is new, nothing is how it's always been done; I got burned a few times doing things wrong—things I should have already known. I learned quickly I had to start asking questions if I wanted to keep the egg off my face.

Asking questions and thinking ahead were some of the best things I began to do. Once a month, I started meeting with a few of the parents who were leaders in the children's ministry, and I began listening to their responses to my new ideas. This gave me great insight into what other people were thinking and how changes I eventually wanted to make would be perceived. The conversations I had with these parents were priceless, and they helped me spin change in the right way when it came time.

They also helped me understand parents' and volunteers' expectations. Some expectations you will never meet, and that's okay as long as God or your pastor has not asked you to, but those expectations still need to be addressed. If people understand the *why*, you can help them understand expectations that are out of perspective.

If you want to lead the people who formerly taught your class and still say things like, "I remember you when you were this big," you better start proving you are a person they want to follow. At a new church you might get away with acting like you have it all together while you are still figuring it out, but at your home church, you are going to have to do a little more than act. These people know you, and chances are they have a pretty solid image in their head of who they think you are. If you want to gain their trust, you need to understand the groups of people you will encounter. The Bible tells us in 1 Thessalonians 5:12 NKJV, "And we urge you, brethren, to recognize those who labor among you, and are over you in the Lord and admonish you." God is trying to tell us two principles about recognizing those who labor among us. The first is to recognize them by telling them you appreciate them, (e.g., get them a gift). The second, in order to recognize them with thanks, you need to recognize who they are and how you can serve them.

There are three groups of people you will have to deal with when leading in the church you grew up in. The first group is the people who have been there forever. They will be your hardest group to lead because they have known you the longest. The second group is the people who have only known you for a few years. They will be easier to lead, and they will find it easier to trust you. Chances are they didn't meet you until you were already becoming a leader of some ministry at the church. The last group is the people who are new to the church or who you recruited for ministry. They probably started trusting you when they agreed to help. Be consistent and reliable to all of your volunteers (no matter how long they have known you) and the children, and they will be faithful to you.

Once you understand these three groups, you will begin to figure out how to earn each one's trust. Sit down and write out a plan of things you can do to gain trust and be dependable to each of these groups over the next year. Then, as you check an item off your list, add one more thing to replace what you have already accomplished. This will keep you always working toward being a servant leader to your volunteers.

One of the hardest things you are going to have to overcome at your home church is getting people to see you as a leader. There are a lot of reasons why people may or may not see you as a leader. Whether or not they are fair is not in your control, but what is in your control is how you address them. Look at Joseph; the situations he was in were not fair, and they were his brothers' fault, but he didn't worry about that. He just kept on doing the right thing by leading those around him and following God's plan.

Remember it's more about what it looks like you're doing, so make sure you look like a leader when you are around people. Dress like a leader. Be on time like a leader. Be prepared like a leader. Step up to the plate and lead. Look, whether people like it or not, God and your church have put you in the position to lead, so be a leader.

I know I do not have all the answers (not even close), and figuring out unspoken expectations is no exception. They are usually not that hard to fix if you find them in time. I really had to grow in the area of asking questions to start to improve on this. I am far from perfect or even great at this, but if you will learn to start asking the right questions, you will start getting the right answers.

When I started working with our children's ministry, I thought I had a good grip of what was going on. There was one program in particular that I knew nothing about, but I didn't ask about it because I didn't know I needed to, but I quickly discovered my mistake when the group of people working with the program did not have their expectations met by me. They probably assumed I knew about the program, and I should have. And once I knew what they expected, it was an easy fix. I could have avoided it if I would have sat down with all the key leaders when I first started and asked a lot of questions about what they needed and what programs we had going.

There are unspoken expectations in every relationship you have except your relationship with God. If you don't learn how to ask questions and find out what those expectations are, you will open the door for some unexpected conflict you could have avoided.

I don't believe ministering in your home church is a lot different than serving at other churches; each has its unique set of challenges. I do believe if you work hard to become a better leader and keep your relationship with God number one, everything else will fall into place. God promises us in Philippians 4:19 that He will supply all of our needs. He didn't say it would be easy or He would keep us in our comfort zone, but He did promise to supply our needs.

Stay faithful to God, your family, and your church; and see what God does.

Chapter 15:
Knowing the Culture of Your Church
Kathy King

The word *culture* is defined by *The Merriam-Webster Dictionary* as "the set of shared attitudes, values, goals, and practices that characterizes an institution or organization." Using this definition, knowing the culture of your church should involve learning your congregation's attitudes, values, goals, and practices. It seems simple enough, but is it?

As ministers, we sometimes live in a separate subculture within the church where we metaphorically eat, sleep, and breathe church. Therefore we aren't faced with the same set of day-to-day issues our parishioners deal with. I have a minister friend who left the local church for denominational work for a period of time. He later confessed trying to make it to church and committee meetings as laity was more difficult than he had anticipated. He realized what a sheltered view of the average church member he had had, and it became clear how different his life had been from the average church member's life. He finally understood what sacrifices a person makes to be active in his church. When he returned to the pastorate, he was much more compassionate and understanding of his congregation; thus, he became a better pastor.

What is the culture of your church? What are your members' attitudes about family life, church membership, or following Christ? Do they value serving in the local church or serving the community and its organizations? Is it important to them to teach their children not only the stories of the Bible but also how to find biblical answers to life's questions? Is church attendance as important as attending their child's baseball game or dance practice? The answers to these questions will give you a good idea of their values. And if you know what they value, you'll have an advantage discerning programming needs and planning when to offer these solutions.

Now that you know the questions, how do you go about finding the answers? John 10:14 reminds us, "I am the good shepherd; I know my sheep and my sheep know me." So we find the answers by knowing our congregation.

And how do we do that? By studying them and their habits. We have to "live among the people" by eating where they eat, shopping where they shop, visiting the ballparks, going to piano recitals, and joining in other activities in which they're involved. We have to sit among them in worship (because of our crazy schedules, something we ministers struggle with this) and cry with them at funerals. We have to celebrate baptisms and weddings with them.

We can study our congregation by talking with them about their interests, by reading about what's relevant to their generation, and by listening to their music. But we must also take time regularly to walk through toy stores to see what's "hot," flip through magazines at the local bookstore, watch kids' television shows, and listen to their music. In addition, we could find out which movies they are watching and who they look up to. According to George Barna's research, the average child spends thirty-seven hours a week taking in mass media. Their lives are impacted quite a lot from outside sources, so in order to know their culture, we, too, must be aware of and involved in these sources.

Interviewing others that work with your kids would be another excellent source for understanding their kid culture. Make appointments to talk with school principals or teachers, dance instructors, soccer coaches, and music teachers. They can give insight into what is on the kids' minds and what type of music they listen to and what their other extra-curricular activities are. And wherever the kids are involved, the parents will be there. Knowing all this helps you understand the issues they're facing.

Perhaps the best way to get to know your congregation is to visit their homes or have them visit yours. In days gone by, it wasn't unusual for pastors to be invited into homes so the members could get to know them. But, alas, those days are long gone, except for within the smaller church communities. If you can't schedule home visits because of either your schedule or theirs, try having individual class gatherings, and spend time at those. This will be a close second to personal, one-on-one time with families. You could even table hop a meal event or wander through the crowd at a picnic.

First Corinthians 9:19 and 22 NASB explain this process for us:

"For though I am free from all men, I have made myself a slave to all, so that I may win more.

"I have become all things to all men, so that I may by all means save some."

This doesn't mean we're to be wishy-washy. Indeed, it's better defined as becoming what we need to be to best minister to the people God has given into our care. "Be shepherds of God's flock that is under your care, serving as overseers—not because you must, but because you are willing, as God wants you to be" (1 Peter 5:2). It is not only our mandate but also our privilege to lead the flock God gives us.

Once again, the question arises, how do we lead our people? Of course, the answer is, by following God's will which is found through prayer. But, let's get real. God doesn't always give an audible reply when we petition Him. Sometimes He uses the influence of others in our lives to help us know His will. Perhaps as we fellowship with other ministers, we may hear about ways God is working in their churches. We may learn from their programming, worship skills, etc., to bring about change within our own congregation. It certainly doesn't hurt to study what our peers are doing and see if things that are working for them might answer needs within our own assemblies. Too many ministers get so absorbed with their own churches that they never see the need nor have the desire to meet with their peers, not only for what they can learn from each other but for the fellowship of being with like-minded instruments of God.

Sometimes a mentoring program or accountability group can show us ways His will can be carried out. Proverbs 27:17 states, "As iron sharpens iron, so one man sharpens another." Through this accountability, we as ministers are encouraged to focus on our own leadership skills, read current literature, and become engaged in dialogues that make us think differently about how we are leading our congregations. Through these relationships, we are forced to modify our ways. We will become better able to help our congregations deal with the inevitable challenges of keeping up with the times.

If we are experiencing growing pains from being exposed to new ideas and new paradigms, we are better equipped to help our congregants deal with such when and if the Lord's leading takes them into uncharted waters. When we realize how painful it is to go about doing things differently, we can help our churchgoers process change more effectively.

Knowing the culture and history of your church can help you navigate these inevitable changes. Older, established churches tend to move more slowly in accepting change, unless they are overwhelmed by an urgent need to change (i.e., overflowing preschool classrooms mean young families are involved. They are the future of the church, so changes must be made to make room for more preschoolers. This will help insure the continuance of the church). Churches under fifty years old may not have the we've-never-done-it-that-way-before attitude; therefore, they may be more open to trying new ways of doing things.

The church in which I have been privileged to serve for seventeen years is 150 years old and is set in a southern, county seat town. I have found that my congregation isn't willing to invest to be on the cutting edge of things, but we will make changes when presented with sufficient evidence that the change is for the good of the entire body. Changes here have to be presented and explained, and then we can proceed.

As leaders, it is our job to help our community of faith remain focused on the path that our heavenly Father places before us. We can influence our people, but only God can change their hearts, minds, and values: "I planted, Apollos watered, but God was causing the growth. So then neither the one who plants nor the one who waters is anything, but God who causes the growth" (1 Cor. 3:6,7 NASB). By keeping our personal priorities in order and by studying the Word, we are better equipped to keep our flock under the leadership of the Good Shepherd. This is a constant struggle but one that is well worth the effort.

Chapter 16:
Copy Or Create?
Jen Galley

Have you ever been to a children's ministry conference that left your head spinning? There you are wandering through hallways full of tables stacked with wonderful resources. Books, DVDs, CDs, games, and everything from puppets to object lessons are calling your name. Inspired and encouraged by the conference speakers, your head is full of dreams and creative ideas about ministry. Your mission is clear—to connect kids from a lost and broken world with their Savior. But just how will you do this?

You've attended workshops on how to:

1. Strategically equip parents to teach their kids at home about Jesus.
2. Create safe, inviting, relevant ministry spaces.
3. Teach your leaders how to invest in a relationship with kids in a small-group setting.
4. Present God's Word in an engaging, never-boring way to every age group from babies to preteens.
5. Improve your processes.
6. Do quality ministry on a shoestring budget.

You leave the conference with renewed passion and a notebook full of workshop notes and business cards from ministers across the country.

Your plane lands back in your hometown. You drive home, pull into the driveway, get out of your car, and open your mailbox. There you find a children's ministry magazine chock-full of great articles and even more fabulous ideas. You quickly realize that Sunday is right around the corner. In fact, the Sunday morning service is always on its way.

Overwhelming, isn't it? You are responsible for leading your team in the right direction. How can you even begin to sift through all of these ideas? Does God even want you to use any of them? Or does He want to give you a new idea? With a limited amount of time and limited resources, how do you decide what will work best for *your* kids at *your* church?

Take a deep breath. Be comforted by the fact that God loves you. He loves the kids in your ministry, and He wants your ministry to succeed. The very best thing you can do in those times is to ask God for wisdom: "If any of you lacks wisdom, he should ask God, who gives generously to all without finding fault, and it will be given to him" (James 1:5).

Now, when it comes down to *how* you will conduct weekly ministry, you have a couple of choices. First, you can choose to copy (buy, borrow, or adapt) the ideas or curriculum that someone else has developed. Or you can create something new.

The longer I serve in ministry, the more I realize that many times the best way for me to spend my time is to purchase resources that have already been developed. If I am behind on being culturally relevant in any area (games, music, etc.), there are curriculum ideas and resources out there that can help bring my ministry up to speed. It's okay to copy ideas and adapt them to my ministry.

There are various examples of trends that can be copied and adapted for your ministry:

1. **Fashion trends:** the kids we are ministering to are a part of the culture. It's good to stay up-to-date with our appearance to be culturally relevant.
2. **Decor:** some of the best ideas for decorating you children's ministry space can be found on TV, in theme parks, at stores for kids/ teens, in magazines, etc.
3. **Design and Publication:** notice the current color schemes, fonts, and graphics being used by large corporations who target children and families. Use these ideas for paint, banners, publications, etc.
4. **Music:** the music you choose for worship, background, and special effects should be culturally relevant and engaging for kids today.

5. **Paperwork:** forms, policy and procedure manuals, and common church business paperwork can be copied with permission and adapted to your environment.
6. **Processes:** check-in processes developed by another church can be used if they fit with your current church.
7. **Curriculum:** not everyone has time or ability to write his/her own curriculum. You can purchase curriculum and spend a bit of time personalizing it rather than doing it all from scratch.

Looking at the list above, the next thing you need to do is to pray about it and ask God what He thinks about which resources, processes, etc., you should use. If you only copy what other people are doing and you skip the talking-to-God part, I guarantee in many ways you will miss the mark.

Does God really care about all of these details? You bet He does. Proverbs 3:5-6 tells us to acknowledge God in *all* of our ways, and He will take care of where we end up: "Trust in the Lord with all your heart and lean not on your own understanding; in all your ways acknowledge him, and he will make your paths straight."

The number-one way to be ineffective in ministry is to be disconnected from Christ who is the Head. (Col. 2:19.) There are so many great ideas we can use from other ministries or from the culture around us, but if we *only* copy others, we will miss the mark.

There have been times when I've read a blog or heard a teaching on how to be excellent in ministry. Rather than praying about my decision-making process, I've simply said to myself, "That's it. That's what I'm going to do. If it works for their ministry, it will work for mine." Like dialing the phone after a late-night infomercial, I've made leadership decisions based on a smart presentation or a feeling of urgency rather than on what God wants to do in and through me. I have been guilty of looking at all of the smart people around me instead of talking to God about it.

The other day, I was trying to turn on a lamp in my living room. I flipped the switch at the top of the lamp near the lightbulb. *Click. Click. Click.* I sat in darkness uselessly turning the knob round and round. I looked closely at the base of the lamp and realized it was unplugged (note to self: lamps do not work when they are unplugged from their energy source). Like a lamp that won't turn on, we cannot be the light that we are called to be in this world unless we stay connected with Christ. Colossians 2:6-7 RSV says, "As you therefore have received Christ Jesus as Lord, continue to live your lives in him, rooted and built up in him and established in the faith, just as you were taught, abounding in thanksgiving."

So, stay connected to the Source. Implementing tricks of the trade will not magically make your ministry great. Do not become distracted by the very tools and ideas designed to help you be effective.

You may be asking, "But what if God wants to do something new?" Yes, we need to be open to creating something new. In fact, in our Infuse group, Bro Jim encouraged us to schedule time to dream. I began doing this, and there are already some ideas the Lord has given me simply because I took the time to talk to Him about it. For example, God has recently given me some ideas about how we can use typical events done at a church (e.g., egg hunts, fall fests, etc.) and equip families to reach their neighbors by hosting some of these events in their own backyard.

Will you join me in asking yourself these questions on a regular basis?

1. Is there a better way to do this?
2. If we could do anything to minister to kids, and if time and budget were not an issue, what would we do?

When you come up with an innovative idea, ask yourself, "Am I the best one to make this happen, or is there someone else that should take this idea and run with it?" For the backyard events idea, I am equipped to make those happen. For other dreams I have involving reaching families through the Internet, I need to consult with other people to see those dreams come true. How about you?

In addition to dreaming, it's important to stay connected to God's direction for your ministry. The **following steps** will help keep you on track.

Step 1: Spend time with God. There's no shortcut for this one.

Step 2: Ask God to help you stay relevant without getting caught up in comparisons or trying to be exactly like another minister or another church.

Step 3: Ask God how to do the best thing for your ministry. God knows the families that you are serving, and He knows how to get their attention.

Step 4: Ask, "Is there a better way to do this?"

Teach your team to be sensitive to God's leading. Encourage your leaders to develop a deep, personal relationship with Him; and periodically ask them to share what He is doing in their lives. Dreaming is a team sport. At every level (greeting, small group, large group, and midweek), check in with your leaders. Ask them, "Is there a better way to do this?"

The best innovators I know are kids. Regularly get feedback from kids to find out if what you are doing is actually effective. Solicit their ideas on how your ministry could better meet their needs.

God has begun a good work in your ministry. As you dream, copy, and create, I pray God will guide your every step so that many will come to know Him.

Chapter 17:
Making Your Leader's Dreams Come True
Beth DeLemos

"He makes the whole body fit together perfectly. As each part
does its own special work, it helps the other parts grow, so that
the whole body is healthy and growing and full of love."

Ephesians 4:16 nlt

The Lord calls us to join together as a unit in order to accomplish our
calling as a church. Every individual's part of the "special work" is going to
be unique because we are all unique. Plus, a majority of the time the "special
work" the Lord calls us to do may not be our own original ideas or even direct
inspirations from the Lord.

When you decided to become a children's minister, the Lord called you to
that position in ministry and planted you at that specific church for a certain
time. There He entrusted you to the care of that leadership and of that pastor.
It is very important that you purposefully choose to trust the Lord and to trust
your pastor is a person that knows how to hear from the Lord. With that said, of
course every person has many weaknesses, and the longer you work with someone, the easier it is to see theirs. But, you must not allow the enemy to do what
he does best—kill, steal, and destroy. You must stay focused on the "whole
body being healthy and growing and full of love."

In order to accomplish what the Lord has called you and your church to
do, you must be on board or hooked up. I know there has been some overkill in
the past years with the armor-bearer and serving messages, but it is extremely
important you take care of the heart issues. You must not just pretend to be on
board with your pastor and your church. It must be a genuine desire to accomplish the tasks that your pastor believes the Lord has led him/her to do. If you
can do this, then you can be successful at making it happen. You could be the
person that gets amazing projects off the ground; it could be anything from a
satellite church, a building project, or even a school. Even if you currently have

no idea how to do those things naturally, the Lord will guide and lead you. When you accept the extras that most likely have nothing to do with your current job description, then He (the awesome Lord God Almighty) will hook you up.

"Why the extras?" you may be thinking. Well, the Bible says in Proverbs 18:16 NKJV, "A man's gift makes room for him, and brings him before great men." Your gift will make room for you. The job description that you signed on for is only a piece of what needs to be accomplished at your church and for your community. Of course, your hired or main responsibilities must not be neglected. Prioritize your responsibilities, and bring on a great team of volunteers to take the journey with you.

Let's continue with a few more heart issues. It is very important that you learn how to arrest your negative thoughts and bring them to captivity. Any negative thoughts or feelings toward any of the leadership you are submitted to can ruin everything the Lord wants to accomplish. Keep yourself clean and pure. Keep yourself connected to the Lord.

Second Chronicles 7:14 NKJV says, "If My people who are called by My name will humble themselves, and pray and seek my face, and turn from their wicked ways, then will I hear from heaven, and will forgive their sin and will heal their land." So many times Christians read this scripture and think it is talking about sinners or those who have not accepted Jesus as their Lord and Savior, but it is not just addressing that. We daily have to choose to seek His face and turn from our wicked ways. Strife, bitterness, and unforgiveness are wicked. If we will choose daily to simply remain in love, then we can be fully used by the Lord. Your gift will make room for you.

> Love is patient, love is kind. It does not envy, it does not boast,
> it is not proud. It is not rude, it is not self-seeking, it is not easily
> angered, it keeps no record of wrongs. Love does not delight in
> evil but rejoices with the truth. It always protects, always trusts,
> always hopes, always perseveres.
>
> 1 Corinthians 13:4-7

Now, on to the fun part! It is time to get excited and ask questions. Spend time with your pastor; find out what gets him excited. Listen to him. Ask him specific questions when he speaks of a dream, a hope, or an idea. You can help get those things in his heart out into reality. So many times, your pastor may not know the task list or how his/her dream could possibly be accomplished—he/she is just able to see the end fruit or the ultimate goal. Many times it will be your job to figure out the natural progression to make it happen.

You can also ask your pastor if you should take on more responsibility. If taking on additional responsibility currently seems impossible, then set the next few months aside to focus on your organizational and management skills. (Jim Wideman is anointed to help fellow ministers with this.)

I am so thrilled that I have had the opportunity to learn and gain experience in many areas of my church. I have had the privilege of working underneath a pastor that is a visionary. He has big, inspired ideas, and when I came on, he was ready for someone to help make those ideas happen. He also has a very laidback personality. In order to be successful on his team, it is absolutely necessary everyone is his/her own self-manager.

About five years ago, when his I accepted this position, I had never experienced this need for self-management. The first area the Lord dealt with me on was redefining my ideas and how I thought things ought to be. I believe if I had not allowed the Lord to shut me up, I would have ruined everything. My gift would not have been a blessing to the ministry but a burden. I was hired to be the children's minister and to work on growing that department. I had the opportunity to fundraise and manage a major renovation on our part of the building. Also I started helping my pastor with a few books he was writing. I took his manuscripts and learned my way by turning those into books, building websites, fulfilling orders, marketing, and doing many other projects. What I have learned these last five years has been priceless. The Word says in Colossians 3:23, "Whatever you do, work at it with all your heart, as working for the Lord, not for men," and I am so glad I didn't just do my job and collect a check. It was worth the late nights and weekends

I am talking about making it happen—at all costs. What does that mean? If God puts a vision in your pastor's heart and then allows you to accomplish it, you don't take no for an answer. You let God show you how to do the impossible by relying on Him for favor and trusting Him to connect you to all the right people.

One of my biggest wins for my pastor happened when I was praying about the children's ministry and about the upcoming planning calendar. I had my eyes closed, and I saw a preschool in the children's department. I saw the teachers in matching uniforms, and I even saw the name of the center. It was so real. I asked the Lord, "Do You want us to start a preschool?"

A few weeks later I scheduled a meeting with my pastor and told him about what I saw. He said he had had that on his heart for a few weeks too. So he had me start researching all the ins and outs and what it would take to get a center started. Once we decided to go for it, I got that center approved by the state, licensed, and opened in less than six months' time.

Every single time it looked like there was no way to get something approved, I did not take no for an answer. Actually, I think I cried in every state office in Nashville. The fire marshal was nine months behind, but because of a connection, he came out one day after we were ready for him. My point is if God is behind the project and/or the vision, He will make it happen through you. You have to trust Him and allow Him to give you ideas and connections to get things accomplished. In the process of establishing the preschool, we met more than ten centers that had been waiting over two years to get approved to open. Now our center is almost full and is a successful ministry to so many families.

Just remember the Lord desires to have your gift make room for you and to bring you before great men. (Prov. 18:16.) He has called you to greatness, and you must trust Him and press toward greatness. It is never anyone else's fault that you aren't moving up in responsibility and effectiveness. That is between you and the Lord your God. Enlarge your tent, keep your heart right, and do great things for the Lord.

Chapter 18:
Walking in Difficulty
Spencer Click

You've been through it before. You come into the office, and your pastor is waiting to read you the riot act. You forgot to finish the job he/she asked you to do last week. Or maybe angry parents sent you an email because they feel like their child has been singled out for correction. Or a board member proposed cutting the children's budget—again.

Any leader who has spent time in ministry knows that sometimes ministry can be painful. Sometimes things aren't fair. Sometimes your spiritual leader or boss is rude, mean, and inconsiderate of your feelings. The reality of ministry is whether you're full-time, part-time, or a volunteer; when you're the leader, it can be hard: "Here is a trustworthy saying: If anyone sets his heart on being an overseer, he desires a noble task" (1 Tim. 3:1).

Read the rest of 1 Timothy 3. The qualities of an overseer are important. These qualities prepare you for the sometimes-harsh reality of what life in a church can be like. Many times I have had conversations with new pastors or leaders about the most difficult thing about being a church leader—people.

It can be heart wrenching and difficult to process when you come to the realization that folks inside the church can be just as mean, rude, and self-ish as people outside of the church. The same can be true of those you work with—administrative assistants, associate pastors, deacons, lead pastors, jani-tors, bookkeepers—anyone can have a bad day and change from a good person to a mean, venom-spewing hydra. When you don't see eye-to-eye with the new executive pastor your lead pastor brought in to oversee you and other staff members, it can make things very difficult.

Sometimes the difficulty we face as a leader is more than just hurtful words or difficult job expectations. At times it can be a genuine spiritual attack (e.g., have you ever had someone question your call to ministry?). Perhaps your church is in transition, and a politically minded individual in the church body is trying to influence the daily operations of the office. Perhaps there is a group of people who are attacking your pastor, making life at church tenuous and uncomfortable. These all are spiritual attacks—someone trying to circumvent the flow of biblical authority to get his or her own agenda pushed through.

Difficult times can make you question your ability to hear God. Difficult times can make you question your call to ministry. Difficult times can change what was once fun into a task and chore. How you handle difficulty and address it is up to you; how it affects you is up to you; how you react to it is up to you; and the choice you make will help to define you as a leader.

I have had my fair share of difficulties in ministry—some I have dealt with well, others have tested my endurance, still others tested my commitment to what God has called me to do. Through the difficulties, I have learned some valuable lessons about how to walk through trials at work and church.

It is easy to assume that all attacks are personal. Harsh words, lies, and criticism all hurt; they can cut to the core of who you are. Though those comments are not always directed at you, sometimes they are merely manifestations of deeper hurts or issues with someone else. Remember, everyone has a bad day every now and then. Give the grace to others you would want to receive yourself, and many things that would normally derail you will fall away.

Ephesians 6 has been so vital in helping me navigate through difficult times. It really lists out for us as believers how we should deal with adversity.

> Finally, be strong in the Lord and in his mighty power.
> Put on the full armor of God so that you can take your stand
> against the devil's schemes. For our struggle is not against flesh
> and blood, but against the rulers, against the authorities, against
> the powers of this dark world and against the spiritual forces of
> evil in the heavenly realms.

Ephesians 6:10-12

"So you can take your stand against the devil's schemes": we must recognize that the true enemy is the devil. He will do anything and everything he can to get you off track. And yes, sometimes he will use Christians to throw you off.

If the devil can get your eyes off of the vision God has given, he will consider it a successful attack.

It is so easy to get distracted from what Jesus has called us to do when we are dealing with difficult situations. We get caught up in the drama, the strife, and the turmoil, but Hebrews 12:1-2 says,

> Therefore, since we are surrounded by such a great cloud of witnesses, let us throw off everything that hinders and the sin that so easily entangles, and let us run with perseverance the race marked out for us. Let us fix our eyes on Jesus, the author and perfecter of our faith.

Keeping our eyes fixed on Jesus will lift us beyond the everyday circumstances of the difficulty. If we keep our eyes on Jesus, we will not become consumed by the hardships we face:

> Therefore put on the full armor of God, so that when the day of evil comes, you may be able to stand your ground, and after you have done everything, to stand. Stand firm then, with the belt of truth buckled around your waist, with the breastplate of righteousness in place, and with your feet fitted with the readiness that comes from the gospel of peace. In addition to all this, take up the shield of faith, with which you can extinguish all the flaming arrows of the evil one. Take the helmet of salvation and the sword of the Spirit, which is the word of God.

> Ephesians 6:13-17

"And after you have done everything, to stand. Stand firm." Are you called to the place where you are ministering? Are you called to your church? Are you called to be a minister? If you are unsure of those questions, then you have to answer them; but if the answer is yes, then you must stand in the place God has placed you. Please don't misinterpret *stand* as *fight*. There's a big difference: fighting is offensive, fighting takes the attack to the enemy, and in a church facing difficulty, going on the attack is like throwing gas on an open flame. Many difficult situations in a church have been made worse by a staff member saying something that was better left unsaid. When you stand, you are trusting God to take care of you. When you fight, you are trusting in yourself. When we remove God from any difficult situation, we are dropping our shield of faith and placing ourselves in a position to face more difficulty. I know it sounds simplistic, but we are the ones who complicate the Gospel, not God.

"And pray in the Spirit on all occasions with all kinds of prayers and requests. With this in mind, be alert and always keep on praying for all the saints" (Eph. 6:18). Pray. Never, never, never, never forget to pray. When we lose motivation, when we feel hopeless, when we feel like there is no answer; we forget the basics. We forget the fact that God wants us to cast our cares upon Him. He wants our burdens. He wants us to cry out to Him. Sometimes it seems as though we aren't hearing anything back from Him, but when we keep our faith up and continue to pray, He is always faithful to take care of us.

Psalm 9:10 says, "Those who know your name will trust in you, for you, Lord, have never forsaken those who seek you." Keeping the words of Ephesians 6 in the forefront of my thoughts and mind has helped me through difficulties. I have come out of trials stronger than I went in. I have grown through adversity, and I am now better for it.

Knowing the promises of God can help you immeasurably, but there are also some very practical things you can do to ensure you navigate through difficulty well.

Galatians 6:2 says, "Carry each other's burdens, and in this way you will fulfill the law of Christ." Let me encourage you to find one or two individuals who can support you and walk through this time with you. There is wisdom in seeking counsel. Please be cautious about who you talk with though. It is never appropriate to seek counsel from congregation members when the issue is a church issue, pastoral issue, or other type of issue that would negatively affect their relationship with the staff or pastor of the church. That is why networking is so important—it provides a wealth of individuals who can be a support for you, but it still allows you to not compromise the integrity of your position at the church.

Sometimes difficult times are more than just a personal thing. Sometimes they affect a whole church body. These are especially difficult. Rumors fly, half-truths become common, and misinformation runs amuck. As a staff member you will have individuals come to you looking for the dirt. RUN! These folks are like flies on manure; they want to know what's happening, but if you lay down with dogs, you're going to wake up with fleas.

Seek God. Earlier I asked, "Are you called to where you are ministering?" If the answer is yes, then you stand. But if the answer is no, then the difficulty you are facing may actually be your fault, so seek God. If He is moving you on, then get ready to go.

Not all adversity is bad. Not every difficult situation is negative. If it draws you closer to God and helps you find His will for your life, then it is a good thing.

Don't spend all your time focusing on the problem. I know it's hard, but when you think of nothing but the difficulty you are facing, it becomes hard to see anything else. Find a hobby, go to the movies, go out with friends—do something that will allow you to not become focused solely on the issue. It can be overwhelming to feel as though there is nothing else in your world but your problems. But to be honest, this is never true.

God will sustain you if you allow Him. You will be okay. Say that to yourself: "I will be okay."

One time my wife and I were going through a difficult time in ministry, so I found myself with a new mantra for that season: "It is what it is." Things were beyond what I could control. I had to trust God because from a human standpoint, I saw no way to triumph over the difficulty I was facing. I lived to tell about it though, and I have found myself more blessed than I ever imagined I would be. If you continue to stand firm, seek God's face, and hold your faith in Him, you will be okay. Actually, you will be better than okay—you will be blessed.

Chapter 19:
Staying True: Being Faithful for the Long Haul
Jon Warneke

Many Americans would know which president was seated in office longer than any other president. However, do you know which president was seated in office the shortest amount of time? If you are like me, you knew the answer to the first question—Franklin Delano Roosevelt, who served as president over twelve years. The answer to the second question was a little more difficult—William Henry Harrison, who was president for all of thirty-one days, twelve hours, and a few odd minutes. Any student of American history can easily list Roosevelt's challenges, shortcomings, and accomplishments. However, the opposite is true with William Henry Harrison. The average American doesn't even know he existed, much less what he might have done in the thirty-one days he was president.

It is hard to accomplish anything of value in short amounts of time. This especially holds true in ministry. It took Jesus over three years of ministry to build up a ragtag team of disciples that would change the world, yet there is no one with a more effective ministry than Jesus. He took twelve men from different walks of life who wore yearbook titles like, "Most Likely to Blow It," "Least Likely to Succeed," and "Most Ordinary Person in Galilee," and He molded them into leaders of the early church. These same men who walked and talked with Jesus over those three-and-a-half years eventually preached sermons where thousands of people came to faith in God; wrote letters, which became books of the Bible; and spoke words that healed the lame and made the blind to see. Along the way, Jesus faced many trials and tribulations, which would have made most people wither, fade away, or quit. Through it all, He effectively ministered to thousands of people. Through the foundation of the people He poured into, that number has grown exponentially every generation for the past 2,000 years.

Do you want to be that effective? Do you want to help mold people's lives?

Do you want to see life change that impels the people under your spiritual care to be world changers? If it took Jesus three and a half years to build an effective, life-changing team, I figure it will probably take you and me a lot longer to do the same. We all want to be highly effective. There are many factors that create effectiveness in ministry, but let me tell you straight—you won't have that experience in the local church without longevity. You definitely don't want to be the William Henry Harrison of children's ministry.

I've had a few crazy ideas in my life, some of them in regards to not being a children's pastor anymore. Since beginning in ministry, I've been tempted (sometimes seriously and sometimes not) to be a rancher, Wal-Mart™ employee, teacher, construction worker, bum, and even a children's evangelist. You know you are having a bad day, week, or month when you begin to think that being a children's evangelist would be fun. There are many circumstances that caused my mind to flirt with trading the blessing of being a children's pastor for some other profession or a search for another more-pleasing or more-fitting ministry position. Let's look a few circumstances that would cause me to leave earlier than God has designed.

Discontentment: I love to run for exercise (it is an acquired taste). My favorite time to run is in the early morning on cool, spring days. In Montana we have *long* winters where white and brown are the only colors we see for months. In March and April we have an annual spring thaw where we begin to see hints of green. This new life fights the elements and begins her yearly journey. By the end of April, everything on the hillsides and fields are a beautiful green. As I run through the countryside, I look into the distance and soak in God's beautiful creation. Everything blends together to form a rolling green carpet, continuous and flowing. It is a flawless and beautiful picture that brings bounce and energy to each of my steps.

But as I focus my attention on the steps immediately in front of me, my perspective changes. In my path, I see unwanted weeds, dry barren patches where the ground is unyielding, and litter that careless people have cast aside. I don't like dwelling on those images, so I turn my eyes back to the far-off fields where everything appears perfect. There is a part of me that wants to run in those fields because they must be so much better. From my vantage point, those fields appear to have no weeds, garbage, or barren ground; but my experience tells me different. I know the grass is not greener on the other side of the valley.

I face a similar experience in the marathon called "ministry." When running through my ministry life, it is easy to concentrate on the things that slow me down and bring discontent: for example, lack of staff, unfulfilled goals and dreams, and simple exhaustion. Conversely, it is equally easy to focus on the beauty I see from a distance in those ministries. There is danger in playing the comparison game. In ministry, just like in my morning jogs, I always come back to reality—no ministry is problem free. Therefore, I must keep my focus and be content with where God has planted me. The Apostle Paul spoke about contentment in Philippians 4:12-13: "I have learned the secret of being content in any and every situation, whether well fed or hungry, whether living in plenty or in want. I can do everything through him who gives me strength."

"I have learned the secret of being content": I am here at God's bidding to do His work. The same one who called me is the one who will give me strength, energy, and determination to finish the course.

Much Work; Little Return: Matthew 9:36-37 tells us, "When [Jesus] saw the crowds, he had compassion on them, because they were harassed and helpless, like sheep without a shepherd. Then he said to his disciples, 'The harvest is plentiful but the workers are few.'" In ministry, we have all been in places where we felt overwhelmed with the amount of work and needs placed in front of us. I remember my first position as an associate pastor. I had been hired to oversee ministry for everyone eighteen years old and younger.

There was so much to be done and, what seemed to be, so little time. I was a complete novice and had inherited all of five volunteers. While parents were telling me one thing, the board would tell me another, and my pastor another. I was completely overwhelmed. At that point, I got a call from a district official in my denomination asking me to direct an area Bible-quiz program. Like an idiot, I said yes primarily because my senior pastor was covering that position and he "encouraged" me to take over. I was a young, green, inexperienced, and overwhelmed individual who didn't know where to begin. At that point, God sent a very wise children's pastor into my life. She sat me down and said, "Jon, pick up one thing at a time, and make sure you do it with excellence. Do that ministry with someone else, train them to do it, and then pick up the next."

In ministry, we can take on so many responsibilities that they bear down and drive us into the ground. We work so hard and often don't see immediate returns. That's where Galatians 6:9 needs to be applied to our lives: "Let us not become weary in doing good, for at the proper time we will reap a harvest if we do not give up." Paul does not say, "If we become weary." Paul emphatically tells us to determine that we *will not* become weary in doing *good*; we are to push through and carry on. To do that, I try not to think about the workload; I focus on the harvest that has been promised.

Trying Times: When writing 2 Timothy 2:3-6, Paul gives the young pastor these instructions concerning ministry:

> Endure hardship with us like a good soldier of Christ Jesus. No one serving as a soldier gets involved in civilian affairs—he wants to please his commanding officer. Similarly, if anyone competes as an athlete, he does not receive the victor's crown unless he competes according to the rules. The hardworking farmer should be the first to receive a share of the crops.

Paul is telling Timothy that soldiers, athletes, and farmers all have to persevere if they are going to receive any reward. If a farmer gives up while preparing the soil, there is no harvest. If the athlete does not follow through, there is no victory. If a soldier worries about civilian tasks, the battle will never be won. If a pastor quits before it's time . . . well, you get the point. When reading the two letters Paul wrote to Timothy, you can surmise Timothy had plenty of reason to feel like quitting. Among the normal ministry, Timothy was facing false doctrine, quarrelsome parishioners, and people who doubted his abilities, calling, and experience. Every person in this world goes through trying times;

extraordinary people overcome them and reap the rewards.

When I showed up for my first ministry position, I had a key member of the congregation walk straight up and ask, "So, when are you going to leave?" As my work continued, I had people ask things like,

"So, are you looking for a new job yet?"

Keep in mind; this was a good church with good people; yet the church never had an associate stay longer than a couple of years, and the record for a senior pastor was four years. Almost every pastor they had ever known had simply used their small body of believers as a stepping-stone to something "bigger and better." So when I ministered there, I worked hard building relationships, restoring trust, and doing things right. I gave the church leadership a promise: "I will not leave until God moves me, and I will never actively look for another position." I planted my family, put down roots, and understood that when I moved, it would be God moving me—not me, not them.

It was the second hardest day of my life—the day when God moved my family and me to a new place of ministry. After four years, God led me to move on. If I had not made that commitment to that church or put down the roots I did, I would never have experienced lasting success or the blessings God poured on my family. I wouldn't now be taking pleasure in the young adults who came out from under my ministry and are now associate pastors themselves; nor would I hear stories of how ministries God used me to pioneer are still going strong with life change happening each week.

Over the years I have lost count of how many phone calls I have received from people calling and asking me to consider positions, often with bigger churches and greater pay. I'm not in ministry for either; I'm here for God's kingdom and his people. When we lose that focus, we lose so much. Pastors quit, falter, and leave way too early. I had a coach once tell me every battle worth fighting would bring a world of pain. The church and community I am in is worth fighting for—bring it on, for in the end I am going to reap a harvest through the power of Jesus Christ.

Chapter 20:
Leaving Well
Jen Galley

Imagine what would happen if you left your current ministry position. Now what if God called you back to serve at the *same* church six months or a year from now? Would the door be graciously re-opened to you by your senior pastor and church board? What would your relationships look like? What would your ministry look like? I know what you're thinking, *That would probably never happen.* And you know what? You might be right, but it happened to me.

In 2009, my husband, Jeremy, and I felt the Lord leading us to leave Oak Hills Church to help start a new church in a nearby suburb. Even though this church plant effort was in partnership with our church, it was still a difficult decision to leave. We had been a part of Oak Hills for a total of nine years. I served as a volunteer in children's ministry for six years and was then on staff for three years. We loved the pastor, the children, and our church family, so we did not take this decision lightly.

We prayed. We sought godly counsel. We listened for the Lord. When we felt that God was directing us to help the pastor of the new church plant, I submitted my resignation. For the remainder of my time on staff at Oak Hills, I worked as hard as I could to set up my pastor, supervisor, ministry team, interim elementary ministries director, and the next children's minister for success. I wanted to ensure that ministry to kids would not skip a beat.

I worked up until the very end with excellence. I was nine-months pregnant, and Sunday, July 26, was officially my last day at Oak Hills. I said goodbye to the congregation from the auditorium stage. After second service, my team threw a surprise going-away party for me. It was a day full of love, emotion, and ice-cream cake. That night our third daughter was born. (I told you I worked up until the *very* end!)

I took a month off for maternity leave. Then I hit the ground running with the next phase of ministry. I had a new baby, a new core team, a new pastor, and a new ministry.

A staggeringly high percentage (over 80 percent) of church plants are reported to fail in their first year. The one we were a part of never really got off the ground. Only five months after leaving Oak Hills, I was more passionate than ever about ministering to kids and families, but unfortunately, I no longer had a church.

In December, I was invited back on staff at Oak Hills Church. These are the exact words of my supervisor. "Jen, because you left so well, I would love to work with you again." Again, Jeremy and I prayed about it, and we felt that God was bringing us back to serve this pastor and church family.

On my first day back, I was so nervous. I had been gone for almost six months. Did I build a ministry that could keep going without me? Would people be glad to see me again? Would they take one look at me and walk out the door? I knew that one of two things could happen. Simply stated,

It would be good.
OR
It would be bad.

Returning to this ministry position could not have gone any better. The team was still serving faithfully week after week. I am so proud of them. I received an amazingly warm welcome from leaders, parents, and kids. Since I have been back, God has increased my team and ministry. And it's all for His glory. It's all about what He is building.

Church is much more than a building, business, or group of people led by a dynamic pastor. It's God's house—a place of worship, hope, healing, reconciliation, and rescue. It's a community, a family. What a high honor and privilege to be called by God to lead and serve in His church: "Therefore, holy brothers, who share in the heavenly calling, fix your thoughts on Jesus" (Heb. 3:1). The beauty and importance of the calling to serve Christ's church far exceeds titles, paychecks, and careers. We get to be a part of what God is doing. Out of His goodness, He allows us to be a part of what He is building. Hebrews 3:4 says, "For every house is built by someone, but God is the builder of everything."

It's important to gain a clear view of what the church is as we explore what it means to leave well. Since God is the one that builds the house, He puts leaders in place. When we listen to Him, He guides our steps. And sometimes God moves us to another ministry position. But it is always with one main purpose—to bring glory to God, the Builder of the house.

People usually remember two things when you leave, first and last impressions. Since church ministry is so important and the community is unparalleled by anything in this world, it can be an extremely sensitive time when God moves a pastor to another job. We are called to be shepherds and overseers of God's people, so it's important that we do everything we can to lead well from start to finish. Our actions should not hinder what God wants to do in the church long after we've moved on to the next steps God has prepared for us in our ministry journey. Christ's church is too special and His message is too important for us to become shortsighted at one of the most delicate times—ministry transition.

If you find yourself in a time of ministry transition, take time to make sure it truly is God is moving you on from your current ministry position. If you are unsure of God's direction, here are a few things to consider:

Check your tank. A car can't run on empty and neither can you. Are you tired? Have you been eating well? How's your home life? Are your priorities in their proper order? Are you connected to your heavenly Father? There's a difference between having a hard season in life or ministry and being released from ministry.

Pray about it.

Seek godly counsel. Use Bro Jim's "Stay or Go?" resource to help you to ask all the right questions.

If God says it's time to go, then go. **Leave in His timing,** and keep as many people and bridges in tact as possible. Ephesians 4:3 says, "Make every effort to keep the unity of the Spirit through the bond of peace."

When you decide to leave, before you resign, you should prepare. Build teams and structure your ministry in such a way that if something happens to you, or if God moves you, your ministry to children and families will not come screeching to a halt.

It is important to **keep the peace**. Tell your pastor first. This is not news that he should hear through the grapevine.

Following your resignation, respect your pastor's wishes regarding communicating this change to the rest of the church. If at all possible, follow your pastor's lead and timetable. Request permission to tell a select few of your closest friends and leaders before a big announcement is made to the church.

From the moment your resignation is announced through the end of your time in this ministry position, be full of grace and show your pastor how thankful you are for this ministry opportunity. Every time you have a chance, thank leaders for a job well done. Thank your pastor for the things he has taught you about ministry. Thank parents for allowing you to minister to their children.

Guard your heart. People say all sorts of things when they feel hurt, disappointed, or shocked. Their reactions don't always match up with their hearts. Believe the best about people, and do not believe everything you hear. Avoid believing the extremes such as gushing compliments (e.g., "No one could ever replace you") or hurtful, cold responses. If you allow it, these types of comments will either puff you up with pride or cause you to sink into the pit of despair. Both are distractions from God's purposes.

Also, before you leave, **set your pastor and team up for success**. Hopefully you have already invested in the people around you, and there are leaders that are ready to step up and fill in the vacancy you will leave. If not, put together a list of your top volunteers that can handle more responsibility. If you do not have time to train them, submit this list with complete contact information to your supervisor so that he or she can contact those people if needed.

Write down everything you do on a daily/weekly/monthly/yearly basis. Make a clear, easy-to-follow chart of the most important routine tasks that must be done in order for ministry to continue. How do you do your job? What monthly and yearly events should the next leader/children's pastor know about? Put this information in a file with all of your leaders' contact information, curriculum website links and passwords, and special instructions. Make a list of where you order special supplies or prizes that will be needed in the next few months.

Prepare your top leaders to fill in during this transition, and encourage your team to continue to honor their commitment to serve. Cast vision for your team. Remind them that God has good plans in store for everyone.

Work hard to the end. Don't just do what you feel like doing. At the end of any job, you may not feel like going the extra mile, but you will never regret leaving well. Colossians 3:23 says it this way, "Whatever you do, work at it with all your heart, as working for the Lord, not for men."

It's a small, small world. The truth is that when you least expect it, you will see people from your former church. Maybe God isn't going to lead you back to a former church to serve on staff, but I can almost guarantee sometime in the future you will run into someone from every church you have been a part of. Maybe you will receive a friend request through a social networking website, or perhaps you'll randomly run into the parent of a child from a former ministry at the grocery store. You could always run into a former senior pastor at a conference, wedding, or funeral. If you don't bump into someone at one of these places, you'll definitely see them in heaven.

Serve God's church well from beginning to end. In that moment, when you least expect it and come face-to-face with the fruit of your ministry, you will know in the deep parts of your heart you have honored the Builder of the house.

Chapter 21:
About the Authors

Spencer Click has served in children's ministry for twenty-three years moving through the ranks as a volunteer-Sunday-school helper to puppet-team coach to full-time children's pastor. He has served at churches ranging from 75–2,500 people in attendance. In 2009, he was named one of the "Top Twenty Emerging Kidmin Leaders" by Group Publishing's Children's Ministry magazine. He and his wife, Heather, currently serve as children's pastors at Bethel Church in Hampton, Virginia.

Beth DeLemos is a developer/marketer who has served in ministry for over twelve years, including five years as the children's minister in her local church. During that time, Beth also put her skills to good use by starting up a publishing house, Bible school, as well as, a preschool. In 2010, Beth joined The Winn Group where she is able to help churches all over the country with developing the tools they need to fulfill their vision. She currently lives in South Bend, Indiana, with her husband, Sam, and their spunky dog, Tilly.

Jenny Funderburke is the wife of a computer geek and mama to the cutest and craziest little girls on the planet. She has served as minister of children at Westwood Baptist Church in Alabaster, Alabama, for over eight years, and she enjoys blogging about kidmin at jennyfunderburke.com. The other loves of her life include ice cream, the beach, and Tennessee Vols football.

Jen Galley has served in children's ministry for over thirteen years, and she is the children's pastor at Oak Hills Church in Eagan, Minnesota. She's highly caffeinated and lives each day to the fullest with her husband, Jeremy, and their three beautiful daughters: Clara, Avery, and Violet. Jen is dedicated to leading families to become fully devoted followers of Christ (www.jengalley.com).

Larry Hillman has ministered to children for almost forty years as a children's pastor, traveling children's evangelist, public and private school teacher, assistant principal, and principal. Larry is currently associate pastor at Faith Life Church in Tampa, Florida, where he oversees ministry departments from birth to adult. He has written several books and recorded several CDs for children to enjoy. He is married to his best friend, and he has four grown children and seven wonderful grandchildren.

Derek Jones is just starting out in ministry, but he has learned a lot of life lessons by growing up as a PK. He is currently the kids' pastor at The People's Church in Spring Hill, Tennessee, where he serves families with children ranging from birth through grade school. Derek and his awesome wife, Tori, recently started their family by adopting a beautiful daughter from Ethiopia.

Kathy King has been minister to children at First Baptist Church of Opelika, Alabama, since 1993. Her husband, Mike, is also her boss as he serves as executive pastor of their church. Kathy loves Auburn University and the beach but not nearly as much as she loves her sweet grandson.

Sean Reece has worked in children's ministry for over twelve years. He is currently serving as a children's director in Texas. He has a wonderful wife and two boys; and all of them love the great outdoors that God has so majestically created.

Sara Richards is currently the Kids' Pastor at Church of the Open Door in Maple Grove, MN. She has been serving kids and families in Kids' Ministries for ten years. She is passionate about developing leaders and about helping kids become more like Jesus. She is married to her best friend, Chad, and they have three boys.

Lisa Walker became a children's minister after traveling for two years in music ministry as a soloist. She has served in churches ranging in membership from

300-2,000. She has recorded two CDs and is currently serving as the children's minister at Lakeview Baptist Church in Hickory, North Carolina. In August of 2010, she completed her certification as a Christian Life Coach and has recently launched Lisa Walker Ministries to accommodate her speaking-and-training events' calendar, as well as, coaching clients. She and her husband, Gene, are parents to three precious gifts from God: Jacob, Joshua, and Sarah; and they reside in Newton, North Carolina.

Keith Warfield got his start in youth ministry and since then has been a children's minister leader for almost six years. He is currently the children's pastor at Grace Church in Fairview Heights, Illinois. He is married to the sweetest, curly-headed brunette in the world. They have the coolest two year old and are looking forward to the baby on the way.

Jon Warneke has been a children's pastor for ten years in his beautiful home state of Montana. He is currently the children's pastor in Polson, Montana. His favorite way to pass time is being outdoors with his beautiful wife and three children.

Jim Wideman is a children's ministry pioneer with over thirty-years experience in the local church. He is currently the associate pastor of Next Generation at World Outreach Church in Murfreesboro, Tennessee, where he oversees all the ministries to families with children birth to college. He is in love with one woman and many guitars. Jim has two beautiful grown daughters, and he is the grandfather of the cutest and smartest baby boy ever born. For more info about Jim, his resources, or his blog; go to **www.jimwideman.com**. He is blessed to have all these people plus a lot more in his life and he's better off for it!

Looking for more information about Jim Wideman's Infuse Coaching program?

Log on to **www.jimwideman.com**

and click on the infuse tab!

For a list of other books and practical ministry resources visit

www.jimwideman.com

Here's what others have said about 'Kidmin Leadership':

"Even beyond the words and messages in this book, the very idea behind this project is significantly powerful. Jim Wideman's books and talks have **profoundly influenced kidmin**. In these pages, you'll read **timeless principles** he teaches that have been put into practice with **much success**. This book should give any kidmin leader **great hope** that if they put these things into practice, they'll see success as well."

–Kenny Conley NEXT GENERATION PASTOR www.childrensministryonline.com

"There are lots of leadership books out there, but when I come across one that is **written by kids' pastors for kids' pastors**, it gets my attention. I love the fact that this book is not full of theories; it is **full of actual experience founded in biblical truth**. Every chapter provides a different perspective that cumulates in one voice calling children's pastors and church leaders alike to up their game and lead; because what we do is eternal, and the Gospel demands it."

–Sam Luce CHILDREN'S PASTOR www.samluce.com

"A book written for leaders by leaders, but not just any leaders—these are ones worth listening to. This is an **incredible resource** that will save young kidmin leaders like myself time, energy, and pain."

–Dustin Nickerson CHILDREN'S MINISTRY DIRECTOR, MARS HILL CHURCH | BELLEVUE CAMPUS www.dustinnickerson.com

CPSIA information can be obtained at www.ICGtesting.com
Printed in the USA
LVOW121652140912

298871LV00005B/80/P